Name _____

P9-DUA-659

INNOVATIONS

The Comprehensive Infant Curriculum:

A Self-Directed Teacher's Guide

The Comprehensive
Infant
CURRICULUM

A Self-Directed
Teacher's
Guide

Linda G. Miller / Kay Albrecht

Copyright

All rights reserved.

Illustrations: Joan Waites
Photographs: Kay Albrecht and CLEO Photography Cover photograph: © 2000, Artville

Bulk Purchase

Gryphon House books are available at special discount when purchased in bulk for special premiums and sales promotions as well as for fund-raising use. Special editions or book excerpts also can be created to specification. For details, contact the Director of Sales at the address or phone number on this page.

Disclaimer

Table of Contents

Introduction

Today, you are beginning a new adventure that will support what you do in the classroom with infants. **Innovations: The Comprehensive Infant Curriculum, A Self-Directed Teacher's Guide** is designed to provide over 40 hours of professional development for teachers using **Innovations: The Comprehensive Infant Curriculum**. While completing the modules in this book, you will have opportunities to explore all the different elements of curriculum that impact very young children and how they learn.

The graphic on the following page shows how comprehensive the **Innovations** view of curriculum is.

Developmental Tasks

Observations and Assessment

Child Development

Interactive Experiences

Teaching

Parent Participation and Involvement

Environment

Activities and Experiences

In addition to exploring the book and learning about all its different features, you will also get a chance to use the curriculum—forms, assessment instruments, activities, and ideas for making toys and materials for the classroom. By the time you complete the **Teacher's Guide**, you will have a thorough understanding of what it takes to plan and implement this exciting curriculum.

The modules in this book are designed to be completed by an individual teacher with the support (hopefully) of a mentor, supervisor, trainer, or director. Each module contains a partial Skills Checklist to assure that things you learn in training are implemented in the classroom and integrated into your teaching skills repertoire. Modules are designed to be completed in the sequence in which they appear.

We hope you enjoy your adventure both in completing this training and in enriching the lives of young children and their families. Write your name on the title page of this book, and let's get started!

Best wishes,

Linta G Miller

Kay Albrecht

Unless noted otherwise, all page numbers in this book are references to
Innovations: The Comprehensive Infant Curriculum.

WELCOME AND PURPOSE OF TRAINING

Purpose: to introduce *Innovations: The Comprehensive Infant Curriculum Teacher's Guide* including assumptions, reasons for teaching, and philosophy of education

TIME: APPROXIMATELY 1 HOUR

Introduction

Innovations: The Comprehensive Infant Curriculum Teacher's Guide is designed to help teachers prepare to use *Innovations: The Comprehensive Infant Curriculum* in the classroom. By using the *Teacher's Guide*, you will be able to learn all the many ways to use Innovations.

Beginning teachers will learn step-by-step about the importance of early care and education for infants. They will learn about basic safety issues, how to create an appropriate environment, how young children learn, and how to include parents in the lives of their children at school. Experienced teachers will have opportunities to learn about new curriculum ideas and to understand concepts of child development. All teachers will be challenged to perfect their skills of interaction, curriculum development, observation, documentation, and assessment.

Assumptions

This teacher-training guide is based on the following assumptions:

* **All teachers need initial, as well as on-going training—no matter what their level of formal education is.** Life-long learning is important for everyone, especially teachers. New research in the area of child development provides insight into how young children grow and learn.

* **Parents are their children's first and most important teachers.** Parents have a stronger and more lasting effect on their children than anyone or anything else. Early attachment determines how safe a child feels, how he feels about himself, and how he relates to others.

* **In addition to their parents, children's teachers are of primary importance in their young lives.** An infant's teacher is a significant adult in terms of attachment and interaction, facilitating emotional and social development. Additionally, teachers have a direct influence on a child's language development through quality interactions.

* **Children's initial experiences with adults are critical in determining how they will relate to others, how they will feel about themselves, and how they will perform academically.** When children have their needs met promptly (when an adult responds to crying in a timely and sensitive manner), they cry less

often. Young children learn that their needs will be met and that the world is a safe place to be.

*** All children deserve to be in an environment where they are safe, loved, and learning.** Early care and education are crucial for all young children. The early years are learning years—especially important for early brain development. Learning windows open, creating an opportunity to stimulate brain development. During these critical periods, children are extremely sensitive to stimulation from interactions and experiences.

*** Being involved in the lives of young children and their families through teaching is an enriching and stimulating experience.** Because "We are shaped and fashioned by what we love" (Goethe), being involved in the lives of young children and their families can be very special and fulfilling.

Why Teach?

Use the space below to explain why you want to teach infants.

What are your beliefs about how you should educate very young children?

_____   _____
Teacher Completing Training Module   Date
(please sign and date)

Congratulations! You have completed Module 1 of 38 in the **Teacher's Guide**.

GET ACQUAINTED WITH INNOVATIONS: THE COMPREHENSIVE INFANT CURRICULUM

MODULE

2

Purpose: to become familiar with *Innovations: The Comprehensive Infant Curriculum*

TIME: APPROXIMATELY 1 HOUR

During this module, you will have an opportunity to get to know how *Innovations: The Comprehensive Infant Curriculum* is put together. (You might find it helpful to create tabs, so you can turn quickly to the different sections.)

Chapter 1—Getting Started (pages 17-29) provides an overview to the entire book. Read the introduction and then find the following sections, which show a variety of what the book offers. Use the Table of Contents (pages 7-12) and the Index (pages 475-495) to find the page numbers.

READ THIS

Page Number	Book Section
_____	Chapter 2—Separating from Parents
_____	Possibilities Plan: Me!
_____	Possibilities Plan: Mommies and Daddies
_____	Chapter 5—Communicating with Parents, Teachers, and Friends
_____	Songs, Poems, Rhymes, and Fingerplays
_____	Blank Forms
_____	Parent Postcards

You will have additional opportunities to get to know the book as you continue with your training.

_____   _____

Teacher Completing Training Module   Date
(please sign and date)

Congratulations! You have completed Module 2 of 38 in the *Teacher's Guide*.

PERSONAL GOALS FOR TRAINING IN TEACHER'S GUIDE

Purpose: to create personal training goals, including goals related to curriculum planning, goals related to observation and assessment, and goals related to child development/specific behaviors

TIME: APPROXIMATELY 1 HOUR

Innovations: The Comprehensive Infant Curriculum is unique in that it views curriculum in a very broad sense. During your training, you will learn about all the following aspects of curriculum that have an impact on infants.

Developmental Tasks

Observations and Assessment

Child Development

Interactive Experiences

Teaching

Parent Participation and Involvement

Environment

Activities and Experiences

As a teacher, it is important for you to set goals. This module will give you an opportunity to do so in specific areas related to your **Innovations** training. You may find it helpful to look back through Chapter 1—Getting Started (pages 17-29) as you write your goals.

My training goal for activities and experiences is to:
(for example, learn five new activities in each Possibilities area, add sensory/art activities to my curriculum planning, or try one project with infants)

My curriculum planning goal is to:
(for example, add webbing to the planning process I use, or invite parents to participate in webbing as part of my curriculum planning)

My observation and assessment goal is to:
(for example, complete one observation on each child each week, or use observations to assess children's development)

My child development/child behavior goal is to:
(for example, understand the behaviors associated with different developmental ages and stages, or help parents understand children's ages and stages and the impact of age and stage on parenting)

Skills Checklist

If you are currently in the classroom, use the complete list on page 95 of this book as a frequent skills checklist to confirm that you are developing your teaching skills repertoire. You may either fill out the skills checklist yourself or ask a teacher to observe you and complete the skills checklist for you (peer evaluation). If you are unfamiliar with an item, read about it in the book or talk with your mentor or trainer. The following is an abbreviated checklist related to this module.

_____Parents and infants are greeted warmly. (see pages 35-36)
_____Toys and equipment are disinfected. (see page 119)
_____Diapering procedures are followed. (see pages 310-311)
_____Quality interactions occur during the day. (see page 233)
_____Safety precautions are followed in the classroom (for example, attendance taken, infants never left alone, chokeable items eliminated, toys and materials regularly checked for safety). (see page 307)

All teachers need someone to talk with and discuss issues concerning the classroom. Individuals can complete this teacher's guide independently, but interaction with a mentor or trainer will make this a more powerful professional experience. Identify the person you will use as a resource in the space below. Consider asking a more experienced teacher, a supervisor, an education professor, a community college teacher, a director, or a consultant from a resource and referral agency.

My mentor or trainer is _____

_____   _____

Teacher Completing Training Module   Date
(please sign and date)

Congratulations! You have completed Module 3 of 38 in the **Teacher's Guide**.

DEVELOPMENTAL TASKS

Purpose: to learn about the developmental tasks included in *Innovations: The Comprehensive Infant Curriculum*, how they differ from other developmental lists, and how to use them while observing infants

TIME: APPROXIMATELY 1 HOUR

Developmental tasks are the very large developmental challenges that children experience as they learn and grow. Most curriculum models focus on the sequence of emerging development. However, **Innovations** focuses on how to encourage, facilitate, and stimulate development. It is interactional, viewing development as the complex interplay between the child and the world. Major interactional tasks are identified and used to construct developmentally appropriate approaches to early education of infants. Developmental tasks in *Innovations: The Comprehensive Infant Curriculum* are loosely sequential from Chapter 2 through Chapter 7.

The developmental tasks of this curriculum are Separating from Parents (Chapter 2—page 31); Connecting with School and Teacher (Chapter 3—page 95); Relating to Self and Others (Chapter 4—page 161); Communicating with Parents, Teachers, and Friends (Chapter 5—page 225); Moving Around (Chapter 6—page 299); and Expressing Feelings with Parents, Teachers, and Friends (Chapter 7—page 365).

READ THIS

Take some time to read about the different developmental tasks in *Innovations: The Comprehensive Infant Curriculum*.

Because developmental tasks are very broad in nature, they often encompass several, or even all of the components of child development (physical, intellectual, emotional, and social). Some people recall these components of development by remembering PIES.

The PIES of Child Development

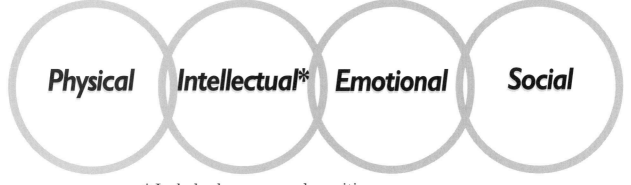

Physical   *Intellectual**   *Emotional*   *Social*

* Includes language and cognition

Read the skills in the developmental task of Connecting with School and Teacher (from Chapter 3, page 97). Label the different boxes as Physical (P), Intellectual (I), Emotional (E), or Social (S). (You will see lots of overlap. The younger the child, the more overlap we see in the domains.)

Infant (0-18 months) Assessment

Task: Connecting with School and Teacher

	0-6 months		6-12 months	12-18 months
C1	a. Does not resist separating from parents.		b. Resists separating from parents; resists comfort from primary teacher.	c. Resists separating from parents; accepts comfort from primary teacher.
C2	a. Accepts transition from parent to teacher.		b. Maintains physical proximity to primary teacher during separation.	c. Seeks primary teacher's support in separating.
C3	a. Comforts after a period of distress.		b. Comforts quickly after being picked up.	c. Comforts when needs or wants are acknowledged by caregiver.
C4	a. Is unaware of friends in classroom.		b. Visually notices friends in classroom.	c. Gets excited about seeing friends; seeks physical proximity.
C5	a. Uses parents and teacher physically to support exploration of the environment; explores objects placed nearby parents and teachers.		b. Uses parents and teacher visually to support exploration of the environment; manipulates objects found in environment.	c. Explores the environment independently; responds to play cues presented by adults.
C6	a. Focuses on face-to-face interaction.	b. Tracks moving object up and down and right to left.	c. Watches people, objects, and activities in immediate environment.	d. Initiates interactions with people, toys, and the environment.
C7	a. Objects exist only when in view.	b. Objects perceived as having separate existence.	c. Looks where objects were last seen after they disappear.	d. Follows visual displacement of objects.
C8	a. Thinks object disappears when it moves out of view.	b. Looks where object was last seen after it disappears.	c. Follows object as it disappears.	d. Searches for hidden object if the disappearance was observed.

Skills Checklist

If you are currently in the classroom, use the complete list on page 95 of this book as a frequent skills checklist to confirm that you are developing your teaching skills repertoire. You may either fill out the skills checklist yourself or ask a teacher to observe you and complete the skills checklist for you (peer evaluation). If you are unfamiliar with an item, read about it in the book or talk with your mentor or trainer. The following is an abbreviated checklist related to this module.

_____Toys and equipment are disinfected. (see page 119)
_____Diapering procedures are followed. (see pages 310-311)
_____Quality interactions occur during the day. (see page 233)
_____Safety precautions are followed in the classroom (for example, attendance taken, infants never left alone, chokeable items eliminated, toys and materials examined for safety). (see page 307)
_____Teacher observes infants regularly during the day. (see pages 19-21)

Teacher Completing Training Module   Date
(please sign and date)

Congratulations! You have completed Module 4 of 38 in the **Teacher's Guide**.

INNOVATIONS IN OBSERVATION/ASSESSMENT

Purpose: to use a developmental continuum for observation and assessment

TIME: APPROXIMATELY 1½ HOURS

The three major goals for observation and assessment are:

Goal 1 To help teachers and parents see children as individuals who have unique skills

Goal 2 To insure developmentally appropriate practice

Goal 3 To guide curriculum development that is sensitive to children's emerging skills, but does not frustrate or overstimulate

This curriculum relies on nonstandardized assessment techniques including:
1. systematic observation
2. anecdotal notes
3. normative checklist

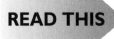

Read the task continuum for each of the developmental tasks. These are located in sections called Innovations in Observation/Assessment (pages 32-33, 96-97, 162-163, 226-227, 300, 366-367). Look at the completed assessment on pages 114-121 to see one possible way to use the continuum for assessment.

Then spend time observing one infant. Perform the following assessment by making three different observations of 5-10 minutes each. Do not mark a subtask unless you observe it.

You will notice that a child may display the behaviors in the box designated for 0-6 months in one subtask, while the same child displays the behaviors in the box designated for 6-12 months on another subtask. This shows the unevenness of development that is typical throughout childhood. Also, notice that you were not able to mark everything. Children do not learn in a straight line. Development is sporadic in nature and proceeds in fits and starts.

To use the results of the assessment, identify a subtask that you did not mark. Next plan an activity (from pages 59-94) or an experience (page 36) that will make it possible for you to observe and assess that subtask.

Which activity or experience did you choose?

What did you observe?

Keep a copy of the assessment (page 33) on a clipboard in your classroom, so you can observe and assess regularly.

Skills Checklist

If you are currently in the classroom, use the complete list on page 95 of this book as a frequent skills checklist to confirm that you are developing your teaching skills repertoire. You may either fill out the skills checklist yourself or ask a teacher to observe you and complete the skills checklist for you (peer evaluation). If you are unfamiliar with an item, read about it in the book or talk with your mentor or trainer. The following is an abbreviated checklist related to this module.

_____Diapering procedures are followed. (see pages 310-311)

_____Quality interactions occur during the day. (see page 233)

_____Safety precautions are followed in the classroom (for example, attendance taken, infants never left alone, chokeable items eliminated, toys and materials examined for safety). (see page 307)

_____Teacher observes infants regularly during the day. (see pages 19-21)

_____Assessment materials are readily available in the classroom (clipboard, pen, forms). (see pages 21-22)

_____   _____

Teacher Completing Training Module   Date
(please sign and date)

Congratulations! You have completed Module 5 of 38 in the **Teacher's Guide**.

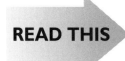

MODULE 6
INNOVATIONS IN CHILD DEVELOPMENT

Purpose: to identify the relationship between infant behaviors and child development principles

TIME: APPROXIMATELY 1½ HOURS

READ THIS

Each chapter includes a section explaining the underlying theory or child development principles, best practices, or content knowledge leading to specific developmental tasks. Child development is under the heading Innovations in Child Development (pages 34-35, 98-100, 164-166, 228-232, 301-307, 367-369). These sections are helpful to teachers as they support children's growth and development. Topics include separation anxiety, primary teaching, literacy development, infant personalities, and social development theories. Innovations in Child Development will show you "why" children behave in different ways.

Often teachers view infant behaviors in isolation. However, infants have their particular characteristics because of underlying child development principles. The following chart shows the relationship between some common "challenges" in the classroom and the child development topics related to them.

Classroom Challenges	Child Development Topics
Biting	Prosocial behavior (page 168)
Aggression	Emotional behavior (page 367)
Crying when Mom leaves	Attachment theory (page 98)
Discipline problems	Guidance and development (page 107)

Choose a classroom challenge with which you need help or one in which you are interested. Read the section referenced that deals with the appropriate child development topic.

How can knowing about child development help with the classroom challenge you chose?

Skills Checklist

If you are currently in the classroom, use the complete list on page 95 of this book as a frequent skills checklist to confirm that you are developing your teaching skills repertoire. You may either fill out the skills checklist yourself or ask a teacher to observe you and complete the skills checklist for you (peer evaluation). If you are unfamiliar with an item, read about it in the book or talk with your mentor or trainer. The following is an abbreviated checklist related to this module.

_____Quality interactions occur during the day. (see page 233)
_____Safety precautions are followed in the classroom (for example, attendance taken, infants never left alone, chokeable items eliminated, toys and materials examined for safety). (see page 307)
_____Teacher observes infants regularly during the day. (see pages 19-21)
_____Assessment materials are readily available in the classroom (clipboard, pen, forms). (see pages 21-22)
_____Teacher explores and discovers the relationship between behavior and child development principles. (see page 34)

_____   _____

Teacher Completing Training Module   Date
(please sign and date)

Congratulations! You have completed Module 6 of 38 in the **Teacher's Guide**.

INNOVATIONS IN INTERACTIVE EXPERIENCES

Purpose: to learn how to plan and use routine times to provide quality interactions for infants

TIME: APPROXIMATELY 1 HOUR

This curriculum advocates thinking about and planning for everything that can, by the nature of the setting (school vs. home), contribute to a child's development and the teacher's relationship with the child and family.

The sections Innovations in Interactive Experiences are a necessary part of the curriculum plan and include types of experiences you, as the teacher, must observe, plan, support, and provide.

READ THIS

Much of the day for infants and their teachers is spent in routine care (diapering, feeding, napping). So, when thinking about time for quality interactions between infants and adults, we might think "when?" The answer to that question is during routine times. Read the following list of experiences (from Chapter 2, page 36). Similar lists of experiences are included in each chapter under Innovations in Interactive Experiences (pages 35-36, 101, 166-167, 233-234, 307-308, 369-370).

Think about the following list of experiences, and make sure that the classroom reflects many of them.

- ☐ Prepare children for transitions. Until they have a great deal more experience with change, infants will struggle each time there is a transition. Talk to infants about what is going to happen to them next and tell them what is happening as it happens (or unfolds).

- ☐ Leave a written record. Leave a written record for the teacher who is covering breaks or at the end of the day. This can take the form of a Communication Sheet (see Appendix pages 428-429) or a spiral notebook with notes about what the child might need next.

- ☐ Watch the tone of your voice and your non-verbal cues during interactions. Match what you say with the way you say it and what you do with the way you do it.

- ☐ Support children as they experience new stimuli. When new things are happening in the school environment, infants need support in taking in the new stimuli. Sometimes this support is preparatory—like warning a baby that the fire alarm is going to go off in a minute and make a loud noise, or reminding children that you are going to pick them up from a comfortable position to move them to the stroller for a ride.

☐ Use routines as a pleasant time for interaction and learning. Take time with diapering, feeding, and playing together. These intimate moments require connections and warm interactions.

☐ Provide support physically as well as visually as new things are experienced. Regardless of temperament, children benefit from being close to someone whom they trust while new experiences are being offered.

By planning for quality interactions, you can use all the time during the day to support children's growth and development.

Look in the Possibilities Plan: Me (pages 59-76) and Possibilities Plan: Mommies and Daddies (pages 77-94) to see what specific activities are appropriate to ensure that the experiences occur during the day. Write the title of the activities under the experience they match.

READ THIS

Skills Checklist

If you are currently in the classroom, use the complete list on page 95 of this book as a frequent skills checklist to confirm that you are developing your teaching skills repertoire. You may either fill out the skills checklist yourself or ask a teacher to observe you and complete the skills checklist for you (peer evaluation). If you are unfamiliar with an item, read about it in the book or talk with your mentor or trainer. The following is an abbreviated checklist related to this module.

_____Safety precautions are followed in the classroom (for example, attendance taken, infants never left alone, chokeable items eliminated, toys and materials examined for safety). (see page 307)
_____Teacher observes infants regularly during the day. (see pages 19-21)
_____Assessment materials are readily available in the classroom (clipboard, pen, forms). (see pages 21-22)
_____Teacher explores and discovers the relationship between behavior and child development principles. (see page 34)
_____Teacher uses routine times to provide individual quality interactions for infants. (see pages 35-36)

_____   _____
Teacher Completing Training Module   Date
(please sign and date)

Congratulations! You have completed Module 7 of 38 in the *Teacher's Guide*.

READ THIS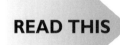

Purpose: to support the development of teacher competencies by using the Innovations in Teaching sections in the chapters

TIME: APPROXIMATELY 1 HOUR

Each chapter contains a section called Innovations in Teaching (pages 37-41, 102-108, 167-176, 234-243, 308-318, 370-383). In these sections, you learn about issues that are important in the classroom. Also included in the section is a checklist entitled Teacher Competencies that you can use to evaluate yourself. You may also use the checklist for peer evaluation or evaluation by a mentor or trainer. Resources for Teachers contains additional reading for teachers.

Read Innovations in Teaching in Chapter 2 (pages 37-47), then complete the following activity. Observe one child in your classroom or in another available classroom. Mark each item on the continuum to the right. Behaviors are described on a continuum from low to high.

Infant Temperament Chart

Nine character traits have been identified to gauge a child's temperament and to help determine the most effective method of caring for each child:

1) activity level

2) regularity of biological rhythms

   (sleeping, eating, and elimination)

3) approach/withdrawal tendencies

4) mood, positive to negative

5) intensity of reaction

6) adaptability

7) sensitivity to light, touch, taste,

   sound, and sights

8) distractibility, and

9) persistence

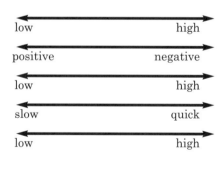
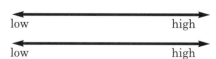

Use the results to determine if the child is primarily flexible, fearful, or feisty. Discuss your findings with your mentor or trainer.

The Teacher Competencies in each chapter are useful for self-evaluation or evaluation by a mentor or trainer. Use the list of Teacher Competencies from Chapter 2 above to rate yourself on behaviors that support children as they separate from parents. Mark the box labeled sometimes, usually, or always for each competency.

Teacher Competencies to Support Separating from Parents

Sometimes	Usually	Always	
☐	☐	☐	Looks up, acknowledges, and greets children and parents as they arrive in the classroom.
☐	☐	☐	Facilitates child's entry into the classroom and separation from parents as they leave.
☐	☐	☐	Accepts and respects each child as she is. Indicates this respect by talking about what is going to happen and waiting for indications of wants or needs before responding.
☐	☐	☐	Shows an awareness of each child's temperament and level of development.
☐	☐	☐	Responds quickly to children who need attention.
☐	☐	☐	Allows children to follow their own schedules; changes with the children as schedules fluctuate. Is an alert observer of each child in the classroom.
☐	☐	☐	Uses routines of eating, resting, and diapering as opportunities to maximize reciprocal interactions.
☐	☐	☐	Monitors children's general comfort and health (for example, warmth, dryness, noses wiped, wet clothes changed, and so on).
☐	☐	☐	Invests in quality time with infants throughout the day during routines and stimulation activities.
☐	☐	☐	Uses floor time to build relationships with children.
☐	☐	☐	Maintains a positive, pleasant attitude toward parents; thinks in terms of creating a partnership to support the child.
☐	☐	☐	Communicates regularly with parents about the child's experience at school; uses a variety of techniques to keep communication flowing freely.
☐	☐	☐	Plans, implements, and evaluates regular parent participation experiences, parent/teacher conferences, and parent education experiences.
☐	☐	☐	Supports children's developing awareness by talking about families, displaying families' photographs, and celebrating accomplishments.
☐	☐	☐	Uses books, pictures, and stories to help children identify with events that occur in the world of the family and the school

Select one competency you feel needs improvement. Make a plan to improve it and discuss your plan with your mentor.

Skills Checklist

If you are currently in the classroom, use the complete list on page 95 of this book as a frequent skills checklist to confirm that you are developing your teaching skills repertoire. You may either fill out the skills checklist yourself or ask a teacher to observe you and complete the skills checklist for you (peer evaluation). If you are unfamiliar with an item, read about it in the book or talk with your mentor or trainer. The following is an abbreviated checklist related to this module.

_____Teacher observes infants regularly during the day. (see pages 19-21)

_____Assessment materials are readily available in the classroom (clipboard, pen, forms). (see pages 21-22)

_____Teacher explores and discovers the relationship between behavior and child development principles. (see page 34)

_____Teacher uses routine times to provide individual quality interactions for infants. (see pages 35-36)

_____Teacher uses reflection to assess and improve teaching competencies. (see page 23)

_____   _____

Teacher Completing Training Module   Date
(please sign and date)

Congratulations! You have completed Module 8 of 38 in the **Teacher's Guide**.

INNOVATIONS IN PARENT PARTNERSHIPS

Purpose: to create partnerships between teachers and parents

TIME: APPROXIMATELY 1 HOUR

Parents, more than any other person, influence the children in your care. No matter how long infants are in group care during the day, their parents are still their primary educators and their child's first and most important teachers. By keeping parents informed, listening to their concerns, and welcoming them to participate in their child's experiences at school, you are able to form partnerships to strengthen families and support children's learning.

Innovations: The Comprehensive Infant Curriculum provides many different ways to develop partnerships with parents and encourage them to participate in their child's life at school. Each chapter includes a section called Innovations in Parent Partnerships that makes suggestions for school-initiated possibilities (such as collecting materials to be made into toys for the classroom), parent participation activities (such as invitations for parents to come to a parent meeting), parent postcards (which include topics to assist parents in understanding and supporting their child's growth and development), and additional resources for parents (pages 47-55, 108-118, 177-186, 244-257, 319-325, 383-386). In addition to all these options, you also can find ideas on how to involve parents in activities and additional postcards in all the different Possibilities Plans. For example, in Possibilities Plan: Me!, see the Parent Participation Possibilities section on pages 72-73 for participation ideas and postcards.

READ THIS

Parental involvement helps everyone. Parents have a higher rate of satisfaction with their child's teacher and their child's school when they are involved. Infants benefit when partnerships are formed between the teacher and the parent. And the teacher benefits from the insight and understanding of the family and the child, creating the best possible situation to support the child in the classroom.

Choose an activity in Chapter 2 to encourage parents to be involved. Write the activity you chose below.

Implement the activity. Then, explain how it worked.

How will you change the activity if you use it again?

Reflecting on the success of chosen parent participation activities allows teachers to modify future plans based on the information and insight gained. Talk with your mentor about your experience.

Skills Checklist

If you are currently in the classroom, use the complete list on page 95 of this book as a frequent skills checklist to confirm that you are developing your teaching skills repertoire. You may either fill out the skills checklist yourself or ask a teacher to observe you and complete the skills checklist for you (peer evaluation). If you are unfamiliar with an item, read about it in the book or talk with your mentor or trainer. The following is an abbreviated checklist related to this module.

_____Assessment materials are readily available in the classroom (clipboard, pen, forms). (see pages 21-22)

_____Teacher explores and discovers the relationship between behavior and child development principles. (see page 34)

_____Teacher uses routine times to provide individual, child-focused, quality interactions for infants. (see pages 35-36)

_____Teacher uses reflection to assess and improve teaching competencies. (see page 23)

_____Teacher supports partnerships with parents through planning and implementing regular parent participation opportunities. (see page 23)

_____Teacher modifies parent participation choices as a result of reflection about the success of planned activities.

_____   _____

Teacher Completing Training Module   Date
(please sign and date)

Congratulations! You have completed Module 9 of 38 in the **Teacher's Guide**.

INNOVATIONS IN ENVIRONMENTS

Purpose: to evaluate important classroom elements that make up the environment

TIME: APPROXIMATELY 1 HOUR

Every classroom has an unusual "extra" teacher. That teacher is the environment. Children learn through the active exploration of their surroundings, so you must plan an appropriate learning environment for the infants in your care. Children in full-day programs have to "live" in their school settings (Greenman and Stonehouse, 1996). Because of this, stimulation activities must be balanced across the important dimensions of activity (quiet or active), location (indoor or outdoor), and initiator (child-initiated or adult-initiated) (Bredekamp, 1997; National Academy of Early Childhood Programs, 1991). Include items from Innovations in Environment on the possibilities plan to add to the environment. Read pages 55-56 for things to consider when choosing furniture and equipment.

Teachers have the following responsibilities for the environment:
* ***Creating the Environment***—Teachers use their knowledge of what a classroom needs to determine room arrangement and the organization of materials.
* ***Maintaining the Environment***—Teachers keep the environment safe by inspecting toys and the classroom for problems. Teachers fix or discard broken toys or toys with missing pieces, and they routinely disinfect toys and surfaces.
* ***Refreshing the Environment***—Teachers plan for different experiences by adding a variety of different materials and taking away some of the old materials. A balance between novel toys, materials, and experiences and familiar toys, materials, and experiences is achieved.

Use the checklist on the following page to evaluate your classroom. Place a check to indicate if you agree, somewhat agree, or disagree.

Classroom Evaluation

Date _____

	Agree	Somewhat Agree	Disagree
Elements are in place that create a sense of calm in the classroom.	☐	☐	☐
Sufficient soft elements help make the environment more home-like.	☐	☐	☐
Appropriate places are provided for babies' things in the classroom.	☐	☐	☐
The classroom is a predictable environment that includes novel and interesting things.	☐	☐	☐
The classroom includes places to be alone that do not sacrifice visual supervision.	☐	☐	☐
The classroom includes places to be with friends (teachers provide changes in scenery, position, and stimulation).	☐	☐	☐
The classroom includes places to be with the teacher for intimate interactions.	☐	☐	☐

Next, use the evaluation to determine a goal you have for improving your classroom. Write it below (for example, create places for each infant to put his or her things, or add some soft elements such as pillows or carpets to the environment).

Skills Checklist

If you are currently in the classroom, use the complete list on page 95 of this book as a frequent skills checklist to confirm that you are developing your teaching skills repertoire. You may either fill out the skills checklist yourself or ask a teacher to observe you and complete the skills checklist for you (peer evaluation). If you are unfamiliar with an item, read about it in the book or talk with your mentor or trainer. The following is an abbreviated checklist related to this module.

_____Teacher explores and discovers the relationship between behavior and child development principles. (see page 34)

_____Teacher uses routine times to provide individual quality interactions for infants. (see pages 35-36)

_____Teacher uses reflection to assess and improve teaching competencies. (see page 23)

_____Teacher supports partnerships with parents through planning and implementing regular parent participation opportunities. (see page 23)

_____Teacher creates, maintains, and refreshes appropriate classroom environment. (see pages 55-57)

_____   _____

Teacher Completing Training Module   Date
(please sign and date)

Congratulations! You have completed Module 10 of 38 in the **Teacher's Guide**.

MODULE 11

ACTIVITIES AND EXPERIENCES

Purpose: to recognize the different types of possibilities (activities and experiences) in the classroom

TIME: APPROXIMATELY 1½ HOURS

Activities and experiences are an important aspect of curriculum. Innovations in Interactive Experiences, a section that appears in each chapter, provides important experiences that you can provide for infants throughout the day.

Additionally, you can find activities throughout the Possibilities sections of the book (Possibilities Plan: Me!, pages 59-76; Possibilities Plan: Mommies and Daddies, pages 77-94; Possibilities Plan: Inside and Outside, pages 121-142; Possibilities Plan: Open and Close, pages 143-160; Possibilities Plan: Big and Little, pages 189-206; Possibilities Plan: Cars, Trucks, and Trains, pages 207-224; Possibilities Plan: Storybook Classics, pages 259-278; Possibilities Plan: Sounds, pages 279-298; Possibilities Plan: Competent Me, pages 327-346; Possibilities Plan: Windows, Walls, Doors, and Hallways, pages 347-364; Possibilities Plan: Senses, pages 389-408; and Possibilities Plan: Bubbles, Mud, and Puddles, pages 409-426). Possibilities Plans are included in and related to each of the six developmental tasks.

Copy the icons on the following page and cut them out. (Enlarge the icons, if necessary.) Tape them to the places in the room where you find toys and materials of that type. For example, tape the Dramatic Possibilities icon to the place in the room where you keep dolls and dishes.

After you tape the icon signs around the room, look to see if you used all of them. For example, if you do not have a CD player and CD's, you probably did not use the Music icon. List below the icons that you did not use.

Now, look to see if you need additional icons. If so, make another copy, cut out the icons, and again tape them to the places in the room where you find toys and materials of that type. List the icons that you used more than once.

What did you learn from this exercise? What will you need to consider in the future as you plan, prepare, and refresh the environment?

Skills Checklist

If you are currently in the classroom, use the complete list on page 95 of this book as a frequent skills checklist to confirm that you are developing your teaching skills repertoire. You may either fill out the skills checklist yourself or ask a teacher to observe you and complete the skills checklist for you (peer evaluation). If you are unfamiliar with an item, read about it in the book or talk with your mentor or trainer. The following is an abbreviated checklist related to this module.

_____Teacher uses routine times to provide individual quality interactions for infants. (see pages 35-36)

_____Teacher uses reflection to assess and improve teaching competencies. (see page 23)

_____Teacher supports partnerships with parents through planning and implementing regular parent participation opportunities. (see page 23)

_____Teacher creates, maintains, and refreshes appropriate classroom environment. (see pages 55-57)

_____Classroom contains experiences and activities that reflect a wide variety of possibilities for children in the classroom. (see pages 24-28)

_____   _____
Teacher Completing Training Module   Date
(please sign and date)

Congratulations! You have completed Module 11 of 38 in the **Teacher's Guide**.

WEBBING

Purpose: to learn about webbing and to practice webbing techniques for curriculum planning

TIME: APPROXIMATELY 1 HOUR

Webbing is a method used to create many different possibilities for activities and experiences and create a picture of the direction in which children's learning might proceed. Through webs, you can provide divergent ideas and identify appropriate knowledge and skills for young children. Each Possibilities Plan starts with a curriculum web. Use these webs as you plan for activities and experiences in your classroom, or make your own webs.

READ THIS

Look at the webs that begin each Possibilities Plan (pages 59, 77, 121, 143, 189, 207, 259, 279, 327, 347, 389, 409). Glance through the activities following the webs to see how they relate.

Create a web of your own for one of the following new topics:

Babies
Picnics
Frogs and Ducks
Stripes and Patterns

Draw your web here.

Skills Checklist

If you are currently in the classroom, use the complete list on page 95 of this book as a frequent skills checklist to confirm that you are developing your teaching skills repertoire. You may either fill out the skills checklist yourself or ask a teacher to observe you and complete the skills checklist for you (peer evaluation). If you are unfamiliar with an item, read about it in the book or talk with your mentor or trainer. The following is an abbreviated checklist related to this module.

_____Teacher uses reflection to assess and improve teaching competencies. (see page 23)

_____Teacher supports partnerships with parents through planning and implementing regular parent participation opportunities. (see page 23)

_____Teacher creates, maintains, and refreshes appropriate classroom environment. (see pages 55-57)

_____Classroom contains experiences and activities that reflect a wide variety of possibilities for children in the classroom. (see pages 24-28)

_____Teacher uses webbing as a technique to support emergent curriculum. (see page 24)

_____   _____

Teacher Completing Training Module   Date
(please sign and date)

Congratulations! You have completed Module 12 of 38 in the **_Teacher's Guide_**.

PLANNING PAGES

Purpose: to practice using planning pages for Possibilities Plans

TIME: APPROXIMATELY 1 HOUR

Each Possibilities Plan begins with planning pages. Glance through all the planning pages included in the book.

Possibilities Plan	Page Numbers for Planning Pages
Me!	pages 60-61
Mommies and Daddies	pages 78-79
Inside and Outside	pages 122-123
Open and Close	pages 144-145
Big and Little	pages 190-191
Cars, Trucks, and Trains	pages 208-209
Storybook Classics	pages 260-261
Sounds	pages 280-281
Competent Me	pages 328-329
Windows, Walls, Doors, and Hallways	pages 348-349
Senses	pages 390-391
Bubbles, Mud, and Puddles	pages 410-411

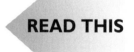

READ THIS

Planning pages are a summary of the titles of the activities and materials with their page references. Often when you are just trying to get some new ideas, you can use the planning pages to glance through and quickly get the activities.

Turn back to one of the Possibilities Plans. Choose two different activities, turn to the pages listed, and read how to do them. Which activities did you choose?

What appealed to you about these particular activities?

Skills Checklist

If you are currently in the classroom, use the complete list on page 95 of this book as a frequent skills checklist to confirm that you are developing your teaching skills repertoire. You may either fill out the skills checklist yourself or ask a teacher to observe you and complete the skills checklist for you (peer evaluation). If you are unfamiliar with an item, read about it in the book or talk with your mentor or trainer. The following is an abbreviated checklist related to this module.

_____Teacher uses reflection to assess and improve teaching competencies. (see page 23)

_____Teacher supports partnerships with parents through planning and implementing regular parent participation opportunities. (see page 23)

_____Teacher creates, maintains, and refreshes appropriate classroom environment. (see pages 55-57)

_____Classroom contains experiences and activities that reflect a wide variety of possibilities for children in the classroom. (see pages 24-28)

_____Teacher uses webbing as a technique to support emergent curriculum. (see page 24)

_____   _____
Teacher Completing Training Module   Date
(please sign and date)

Congratulations! You have completed Module 13 of 38 in the **Teacher's Guide**.

POSSIBILITIES

Purpose: to explore the different types of possibilities in the book and to determine the possibilities and materials needed for your classroom

TIME: APPROXIMATELY 1 HOUR

Read about the different possibilities for the infant room in Possibilities Plans in Chapter 1: Getting Started (pages 24-29). Possibilities Plans contain the following elements:

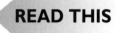

1. Webs (example, page 59)
2. Planning Pages (example, pages 60-61)
3. Dramatic Possibilities (example, page 62)
4. Sensory and Art Possibilities (example, page 63)
5. Curiosity Possibilities (example, page 64)
6. Literacy Possibilities (example, page 65)
7. Music Possibilities (example, page 68)
8. Movement Possibilities (example, page 69)
9. Outdoor Possibilities (example, page 70)
10. Project Possibilities (example, page 71)
11. Parent Participation Possibilities (example, page 72)
12. Concepts Learned (example, page 74)
13. Resources (example, pages 74-75)
    - Prop Boxes
    - Picture File/Vocabulary
    - Books
    - Rhymes/Fingerplays
    - Music/Songs
14. Toys and Materials (gathered and bought) (example, page 76)

Look back at Module 11. What types of possibilities do you have missing in your classroom? Below, write a goal you have for including materials that currently are not in your room. Create a "wish list" for materials needed for your classroom.

Goal for Adding Possibilities: (for example, add sensory, music, and dramatic play toys and materials to the classroom including...)

Wish list for materials you need for your classroom:

Skills Checklist

If you are currently in the classroom, use the complete list on page 95 of this book as a frequent skills checklist to confirm that you are developing your teaching skills repertoire. You may either fill out the skills checklist yourself or ask a teacher to observe you and complete the skills checklist for you (peer evaluation). If you are unfamiliar with an item, read about it in the book or talk with your mentor or trainer. The following is an abbreviated checklist related to this module.

_____Teacher supports partnerships with parents through planning and implementing regular parent participation opportunities. (see page 23)

_____Teacher creates, maintains, and refreshes appropriate classroom environment. (see pages 55-57)

_____Classroom contains experiences and activities that reflect a wide variety of possibilities for children in the classroom. (see pages 24-28)

_____Teacher uses webbing as a technique to support emergent curriculum. (see page 24)

_____Classroom includes a wide variety of appropriate toys and materials. (see pages 24-29)

_____   _____
Teacher Completing Training Module   Date
(please sign and date)

Congratulations! You have completed Module 14 of 38 in the **Teacher's Guide**.

DRAMATIC POSSIBILITIES

Purpose: to understand what dramatic possibilities are and to create a teacher-made toy for the classroom from dramatic possibilities

TIME: APPROXIMATELY 1½ HOURS

Read about Dramatic Possibilities on page 25. Activities of this type are a favorite for both infants and teachers. Look around your classroom or another classroom in your school to see what dramatic possibilities materials are available. Make a list of what you find:

READ THIS

Now, look at one of the Possibilities Plans in the book. Find an activity that describes a dramatic possibilities toy that you would like to make for your classroom. Also, read pages 168-171 for more information on making toys and finding materials.

READ THIS

What toy did you choose?

Gather the materials and create the teacher-made toy. Safety is a prime concern for teacher-made materials, so be sure to check the toy carefully for safety. Also ask your mentor or trainer to check the toy for safety before using it in your classroom.

_____   _____
Checked Toy for Safety   Date

Describe the toy that you made for your classroom.

How do you plan to use it?

Skills Checklist

If you are currently in the classroom, use the complete list on page 95 of this book as a frequent skills checklist to confirm that you are developing your teaching skills repertoire. You may either fill out the skills checklist yourself or ask a teacher to observe you and complete the skills checklist for you (peer evaluation). If you are unfamiliar with an item, read about it in the book or talk with your mentor or trainer. The following is an abbreviated checklist related to this module.

_____Teacher creates, maintains, and refreshes appropriate classroom environment. (see pages 55-57)

_____Classroom contains experiences and activities that reflect a wide variety of possibilities for children in the classroom. (see pages 24-28)

_____Teacher uses webbing as a technique to support emergent curriculum. (see page 24)

_____Classroom includes a wide variety of appropriate toys and materials. (see pages 24-29)

_____Classroom includes a variety of safe, appropriate, teacher-made toys. (see pages 168-171)

_____   _____

Teacher Completing Training Module   Date
(please sign and date)

Congratulations! You have completed Module 15 of 38 in the **Teacher's Guide**.

SENSORY AND ART POSSIBILITIES

Purpose: to understand what sensory and art possibilities are and to create a teacher-made toy for the classroom from sensory and art possibilities

TIME: APPROXIMATELY I HOUR

Read about Sensory and Art Possibilities on page 25. Look around your classroom or another classroom in your school to see what sensory and art possibilities materials are available. Make a list of what you find:

READ THIS

Now, look at one of the Possibilities Plans in the book. Find an activity that describes a sensory and art possibilities toy that you would like to make for your classroom. Also, read pages 168-171 for more information on making toys and finding materials.

READ THIS

What toy did you choose?

Gather the materials and create the teacher-made toy. Safety is a prime concern for teacher-made materials, so be sure to check the toy carefully for safety. Also ask your mentor or trainer to check the toy for safety before using it in your classroom.

_____   _____

Checked Toy for Safety   Date

Describe the toy that you made for your classroom.

How do you plan to use it?

Skills Checklist

If you are currently in the classroom, use the complete list on page 95 of this book as a frequent skills checklist to confirm that you are developing your teaching skills repertoire. You may either fill out the skills checklist yourself or ask a teacher to observe you and complete the skills checklist for you (peer evaluation). If you are unfamiliar with an item, read about it in the book or talk with your mentor or trainer. The following is an abbreviated checklist related to this module.

_____Teacher creates, maintains, and refreshes appropriate classroom environment. (see pages 55-57)

_____Classroom contains experiences and activities that reflect a wide variety of possibilities for children in the classroom. (see pages 24-28)

_____Teacher uses webbing as a technique to support emergent curriculum. (see page 24)

_____Classroom includes a wide variety of appropriate toys and materials. (see pages 24-29)

_____Classroom includes a variety of safe, appropriate, teacher-made toys. (see pages 168-171)

_____   _____

Teacher Completing Training Module   Date
(please sign and date)

Congratulations! You have completed Module 16 of 38 in the **Teacher's Guide.**

CURIOSITY POSSIBILITIES

Purpose: to understand what curiosity possibilities are and to create a teacher-made toy for the classroom from curiosity possibilities

TIME: APPROXIMATELY 1 HOUR

Read about Curiosity Possibilities on pages 25-27. Look around your classroom or another classroom in your school to see what curiosity possibilities materials are available. Make a list of what you find:

READ THIS

Now, look at one of the Possibilities Plans in the book. Find an activity that describes a curiosity possibilities toy that you would like to make for your classroom. Also, read pages 168-171 for more information on making toys and finding materials.

READ THIS

What toy did you choose?

Gather the materials and create the teacher-made toy. Safety is a prime concern for teacher-made materials, so be sure to check the toy carefully for safety. Also ask your mentor or trainer to check the toy for safety before using it in your classroom.

_____   _____
Checked Toy for Safety   Date

Describe the toy that you made for your classroom.

How do you plan to use it?

Skills Checklist

If you are currently in the classroom, use the complete list on page 95 of this book as a frequent skills checklist to confirm that you are developing your teaching skills repertoire. You may either fill out the skills checklist yourself or ask a teacher to observe you and complete the skills checklist for you (peer evaluation). If you are unfamiliar with an item, read about it in the book or talk with your mentor or trainer. The following is an abbreviated checklist related to this module.

_____Teacher creates, maintains, and refreshes appropriate classroom
environment. (see pages 55-57)
_____Classroom contains experiences and activities that reflect a wide variety
of possibilities for children in the classroom. (see pages 24-28)
_____Teacher uses webbing as a technique to support emergent curriculum.
(see page 24)
_____Classroom includes a wide variety of appropriate toys and materials.
(see pages 24-29)
_____Classroom includes a variety of safe, appropriate, teacher-made toys.
(see pages 168-171)

_____   _____

Teacher Completing Training Module   Date
(please sign and date)

Congratulations! You have completed Module 17 of 38 in the **Teacher's Guide**.

LITERACY POSSIBILITIES

Purpose: to understand what literacy possibilities are and to create a teacher-made toy for the classroom from literacy possibilities

TIME: APPROXIMATELY 1 HOUR

Read about Literacy Possibilities on page 27. Look around your classroom or another classroom in your school to see what literacy possibilities materials are available. Make a list of what you find:

READ THIS

Now, look at one of the Possibilities Plans in the book. Find an activity that describes a literacy possibilities toy that you would like to make for your classroom. Also, read pages 168-171 for more information on making toys and finding materials.

READ THIS

What toy did you choose?

Gather the materials and create the teacher-made toy. Safety is a prime concern for teacher-made materials, so be sure to check the toy carefully for safety. Also ask your mentor or trainer to check the toy for safety before using it in your classroom.

_____   _____

Checked Toy for Safety   Date

Describe the toy that you made for your classroom.

How do you plan to use it?

Skills Checklist

If you are currently in the classroom, use the complete list on page 95 of this book as a frequent skills checklist to confirm that you are developing your teaching skills repertoire. You may either fill out the skills checklist yourself or ask a teacher to observe you and complete the skills checklist for you (peer evaluation). If you are unfamiliar with an item, read about it in the book or talk with your mentor or trainer. The following is an abbreviated checklist related to this module.

_____Teacher creates, maintains, and refreshes appropriate classroom environment. (see pages 55-57)

_____Classroom contains experiences and activities that reflect a wide variety of possibilities for children in the classroom. (see pages 24-28)

_____Teacher uses webbing as a technique to support emergent curriculum. (see page 24)

_____Classroom includes a wide variety of appropriate toys and materials. (see pages 24-29)

_____Classroom includes a variety of safe, appropriate, teacher-made toys. (see pages 168-171)

_____   _____

Teacher Completing Training Module   Date
(please sign and date)

Congratulations! You have completed Module 18 of 38 in the **Teacher's Guide**.

MUSIC POSSIBILITIES

Purpose: to understand what music possibilities are and to create a teacher-made toy for the classroom from music possibilities

TIME: APPROXIMATELY I HOUR

Read about Music Possibilities on page 27. Look around your classroom or another classroom in your school to see what music possibilities materials are available. Make a list of what you find:

READ THIS

Now, look at one of the Possibilities Plans in the book. Find an activity that describes a music possibilities toy that you would like to make for your classroom. Also, read pages 168-171 for more information on making toys and finding materials.

READ THIS

What toy did you choose?

Gather the materials and create the teacher-made toy. Safety is a prime concern for teacher-made materials, so be sure to check the toy carefully for safety. Also ask your mentor or trainer to check the toy for safety before using it in your classroom.

_____   _____

Checked Toy for Safety   Date

Describe the toy that you made for your classroom.

How do you plan to use it?

Skills Checklist

If you are currently in the classroom, use the complete list on page 95 of this book as a frequent skills checklist to confirm that you are developing your teaching skills repertoire. You may either fill out the skills checklist yourself or ask a teacher to observe you and complete the skills checklist for you (peer evaluation). If you are unfamiliar with an item, read about it in the book or talk with your mentor or trainer. The following is an abbreviated checklist related to this module.

_____Teacher creates, maintains, and refreshes appropriate classroom environment. (see pages 55-57)

_____Classroom contains experiences and activities that reflect a wide variety of possibilities for children in the classroom. (see pages 24-28)

_____Teacher uses webbing as a technique to support emergent curriculum. (see pages 24)

_____Classroom includes a wide variety of appropriate toys and materials. (see pages 24-29)

_____Classroom includes a variety of safe, appropriate, teacher-made toys. (see pages 168-171)

_____   _____

Teacher Completing Training Module   Date
(please sign and date)

Congratulations! You have completed Module 19 of 38 in the **Teacher's Guide**.

MOVEMENT POSSIBILITIES

Purpose: to understand what movement possibilities are and to create a teacher-made toy for the classroom from movement possibilities

TIME: APPROXIMATELY 1 HOUR

Read about Movement Possibilities on pages 27-28. Look around your classroom or another classroom in your school to see what movement possibilities materials are available. Make a list of what you find:

READ THIS

Now, look at one of the Possibilities Plans in the book. Find an activity that describes a movement possibilities toy that you would like to make for your classroom. Also, read pages 168-171 for more information on making toys and finding materials.

READ THIS

What toy did you choose?

Gather the materials and create the teacher-made toy. Safety is a prime concern for teacher-made materials, so be sure to check the toy carefully for safety. Also ask your mentor or trainer to check the toy for safety before using it in your classroom.

_____   _____

Checked Toy for Safety   Date

Describe the toy that you made for your classroom.

How do you plan to use it?

Skills Checklist

If you are currently in the classroom, use the complete list on page 95 of this book as a frequent skills checklist to confirm that you are developing your teaching skills repertoire. You may either fill out the skills checklist yourself or ask a teacher to observe you and complete the skills checklist for you (peer evaluation). If you are unfamiliar with an item, read about it in the book or talk with your mentor or trainer. The following is an abbreviated checklist related to this module.

_____Teacher creates, maintains, and refreshes appropriate classroom environment. (see pages 55-57)

_____Classroom contains experiences and activities that reflect a wide variety of possibilities for children in the classroom. (see pages 24-28)

_____Teacher uses webbing as a technique to support emergent curriculum. (see page 24)

_____Classroom includes a wide variety of appropriate toys and materials. (see pages 24-29)

_____Classroom includes a variety of safe, appropriate, teacher-made toys. (see pages 168-171)

_____   _____

Teacher Completing Training Module   Date
(please sign and date)

Congratulations! You have completed Module 20 of 38 in the **Teacher's Guide**.

OUTDOOR POSSIBILITIES

Purpose: to understand what outdoor possibilities are and to create a teacher-made toy for the classroom from outdoor possibilities

TIME: APPROXIMATELY I HOUR

Read about Outdoor Possibilities on page 28. Look around your classroom or another classroom in your school to see what outdoor possibilities materials are available. Make a list of what you find:

READ THIS

Now, look at one of the Possibilities Plans in the book. Find an activity that describes an outdoor possibilities toy that you would like to make. Also, read pages 168-171 for more information on making toys and finding materials.

READ THIS

What toy did you choose?

Gather the materials and create the teacher-made toy. Safety is a prime concern for teacher-made materials, so be sure to check the toy carefully for safety. Also ask your mentor or trainer to check the toy for safety before using it in your classroom.

_____   _____

Checked Toy for Safety   Date

Describe the toy that you made for the outside.

How do you plan to use it?

Skills Checklist

If you are currently in the classroom, use the complete list on page 95 of this book as a frequent skills checklist to confirm that you are developing your teaching skills repertoire. You may either fill out the skills checklist yourself or ask a teacher to observe you and complete the skills checklist for you (peer evaluation). If you are unfamiliar with an item, read about it in the book or talk with your mentor or trainer. The following is an abbreviated checklist related to this module.

_____Teacher creates, maintains, and refreshes appropriate classroom environment. (see pages 55-57)

_____Classroom contains experiences and activities that reflect a wide variety of possibilities for children in the classroom. (see pages 24-28)

_____Teacher uses webbing as a technique to support emergent curriculum. (see page 24)

_____Classroom includes a wide variety of appropriate toys and materials. (see pages 24-29)

_____Classroom includes a variety of safe, appropriate, teacher-made toys. (see pages 168-171)

_____   _____
Teacher Completing Training Module   Date
(please sign and date)

Congratulations! You have completed Module 21 of 38 in the **Teacher's Guide**.

PROJECT POSSIBILITIES

Purpose: to understand project possibilities and to plan one for the classroom

TIME: APPROXIMATELY 1 HOUR

Projects are repeated experiences that children have over time. (Activities that last one day or even a week probably are not projects.) By including projects in children's experiences, you can give children a sense of familiarity and security because activities are revisited. Read about projects in Getting Started on page 28. Then read about the project Wrapping Paper for Parents on page 421.

Each Possibilities Plan includes ideas for projects. Look on the planning pages or even in the table of contents to find the Project Possibilities.

Choose an activity from anywhere in the Possibilities Plan sections of the book and turn the activity into a project.

What activity did you choose? Write the title below with the page number.

How can you turn this activity into a project for infants?

Try the project with the infants in your classroom. Write what happened below.

Skills Checklist

If you are currently in the classroom, use the complete list on page 95 of this book as a frequent skills checklist to confirm that you are developing your teaching skills repertoire. You may either fill out the skills checklist yourself or ask a teacher to observe you and complete the skills checklist for you (peer evaluation). If you are unfamiliar with an item, read about it in the book or talk with your mentor or trainer. The following is an abbreviated checklist related to this module.

_____Classroom contains experiences and activities that reflect a wide variety of possibilities for children in the classroom. (see pages 24-28)

_____Teacher uses webbing as a technique to support emergent curriculum. (see page 24)

_____Classroom includes a wide variety of appropriate toys and materials. (see pages 24-29)

_____Classroom includes a variety of safe, appropriate, teacher-made toys. (see pages 168-171)

_____Teacher uses projects to provide repeated experiences over time for infants. (see page 28)

_____   _____

Teacher Completing Training Module   Date
(please sign and date)

Congratulations! You have completed Module 22 of 38 in the **Teacher's Guide**.

PARENT PARTICIPATION POSSIBILITIES

Purpose: to learn about, plan, and implement parent participation activities that will help support parent partnerships

TIME: APPROXIMATELY 1 HOUR

Parents are so important in the lives of their children, and teachers are in a position to support them by creating partnerships with parents. *Innovations: The Comprehensive Infant Curriculum* has numerous ideas to help you in that role.

Each chapter contains a section called Innovations in Parent Partnerships, which includes suggestions for school-initiated possibilities (such as collecting materials to be made into toys for the classroom), parent participation activities (such as invitations for parents to come to a parent meeting), parent postcards to give to parents (which include topics to assist parents in understanding and supporting their child's growth and development), and additional resources for parents (pages 47-55, 108-118, 177-186, 244-257, 319-325, 383-386). In addition to all these options, you also can find ideas on how to get parents involved in activities and additional postcards in all the different Possibilities Plans. For example, in Possibilities Plan: Me!, see the Parent Participation Possibilities section on pages 72-73 for participation ideas and postcards.

READ THIS

To support partnerships with parents, plan activities for parents for the next two weeks. What ideas have you chosen? Write them below.

How will you communicate with parents about these activities?

How will you prepare for the events?

How did the planned events go?

What will you do differently next time?

Skills Checklist

If you are currently in the classroom, use the complete list on page 95 of this book as a frequent skills checklist to confirm that you are developing your teaching skills repertoire. You may either fill out the skills checklist yourself or ask a teacher to observe you and complete the skills checklist for you (peer evaluation). If you are unfamiliar with an item, read about it in the book or talk with your mentor or trainer. The following is an abbreviated checklist related to this module.

_____Classroom contains experiences and activities that reflect a wide variety of possibilities for children in the classroom. (see pages 24-28)

_____Teacher uses webbing as a technique to support emergent curriculum. (see page 24)

_____Classroom includes a wide variety of appropriate toys and materials. (see pages 24-29)

_____Classroom includes a variety of safe, appropriate, teacher-made toys. (see pages 168-171)

_____Teacher uses projects to provide repeated experiences over time for infants. (see pages 28)

_____Teacher plans, implements, and evaluates the success of parent participation activities.

_____   _____

Teacher Completing Training Module   Date
(please sign and date)

Congratulations! You have completed Module 23 of 38 in the **Teacher's Guide**.

CONCEPTS LEARNED

Purpose: to explain how to use Concepts Learned in the Classroom and how to use these lists as one way to communicate to parents about their child's experiences in the classroom

TIME: APPROXIMATELY 1 HOUR

It is often difficult for parents to see the important interactive experiences that infants are having in school as learning activities. **Innovations: The Comprehensive Infant Curriculum** has a strategy for helping you share with parents what children are learning. Concepts Learned lists are provided for each Possibilities Plan, and you can use these lists in a variety of ways.

The easiest way to use the Concepts Learned list is to copy the appropriate list from the appendix and post it in the classroom. When posted, parents will be able to see the content and process learning that is taking place in your classroom.

To make the list come alive for individual children and their parents, use the list to document children's learning. For example, using the Concepts Learned list from the Mommies and Daddies Possibilities Plan (page 92), you might put the child's name and date next to the concept learned by each child.

Example:
    Mommies and daddies come back. *Julia, 10/5*
    A child has a mommy and a daddy.
    Mommies and daddies are special. *Kerry, 9/8*
    Mommies and daddies do different things.
    Families love babies and help them.
    Mommies and daddies garden, cook, clean, work, and camp out.
    Textures feel different.
    I can pretend. *Lucy, 10/14*
    Mommies and daddies have car keys. *Cindy, 9/30*
    Pots and pans have lids.
    Picnic baskets are full of stuff!
    Things float.
    I can shake a rattle. *Mike, 10/26*
    I can dig in the dirt.
    I can turn the pages in a book. *Jalen, 11/1*
    I can clean.
    I can use the telephone.
    I can empty and fill the picnic basket. *Sun Li, 10/18*

You might choose to edit the list from the book, adding additional concepts learned from other experiences provided by you. You may also find it helpful to number the concepts on a Concepts Learned list and then use these numbers when completing anecdotal observations.

Concepts Learned are important for parents because they let them know what you and their child have been doing and what the results are. Concepts are very simple—relating to things that infants can understand. Both content and process knowledge are included. For example, using the Concepts Learned list for Mommies and Daddies (page 92), one example of content knowledge is "Picnic baskets are full of stuff," and one example of process knowledge is "I can pretend."

Select a Concepts Learned list from the appendix. Observe a classroom for about 15-20 minutes, using the list to assess what children are learning. Add additional items to the list that become apparent during your observation. Discuss your observation with your mentor or trainer.

List the items that you added to Concepts Learned.

Observation discussed with _____ .
                (Name)   (Date)

Skills Checklist

If you are currently in the classroom, use the complete list on page 95 of this book as a frequent skills checklist to confirm that you are developing your teaching skills repertoire. You may either fill out the skills checklist yourself or ask a teacher to observe you and complete the skills checklist for you (peer evaluation). If you are unfamiliar with an item, read about it in the book or talk with your mentor or trainer. The following is an abbreviated checklist related to this module.

_____Classroom includes a wide variety of appropriate toys and materials. (see pages 24-28)

_____Classroom includes a variety of safe, appropriate, teacher-made toys. (see pages 168-171)

_____Teacher uses projects to provide repeated experiences over time for infants. (see page 28)

_____Teacher plans, implements, and evaluates the success of parent participation activities.

_____Teacher uses Concepts Learned to communicate with parents about their children. (see pages 28-29, 452-463)

_____   _____

Teacher Completing Training Module   Date
(please sign and date)

Congratulations! You have completed Module 24 of 38 in the **Teacher's Guide**.

RESOURCES

Purpose: to explore the resources sections of the book to support learning for infants

TIME: APPROXIMATELY 1 HOUR

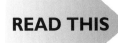

READ THIS

Read about the resources available to you to support learning for infants (page 29). Then look through one of the resources sections in the book found in each Possibilities Plan (pages 74-76 in ME!; pages 92-94 in Mommies and Daddies; pages 139-141 in Inside and Outside; pages 158-160 in Open and Close; pages 205-206 in Big and Little; pages 222-224 in Cars, Trucks, and Trains; pages 276-278 in Storybook Classics; pages 296-298 in Sounds; pages 343-346 in Competent Me; pages 362-364 in Windows, Walls, Doors, and Hallways; pages 405-407 in Senses; pages 425-426 in Bubbles, Mud, and Puddles).

After reading one of the resources sections, practice filling out a Possibilities Plan. Use the partial section of a blank Possibilities Plan below and write in the appropriate sections what you have chosen from the resources section. See pages 450-451 for an example.

Dramatic Possibilities	
Art/Sensory Possibilities	
Curiosity Possibilities	
Music Possibilities	
Movement Possibilities	
Literacy Possibilities	
Outdoor Possibilities	
Project Possibilities	

Books	Picture File Pictures/Vocabulary

Rhymes & Fingerplays	Music/Songs	Prop Boxes

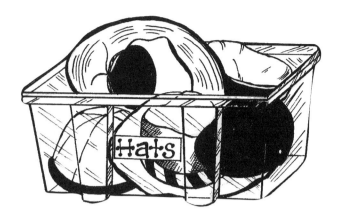

Skills Checklist

If you are currently in the classroom, use the complete list on page 95 of this book as a frequent skills checklist to confirm that you are developing your teaching skills repertoire. You may either fill out the skills checklist yourself or ask a teacher to observe you and complete the skills checklist for you (peer evaluation). If you are unfamiliar with an item, read about it in the book or talk with your mentor or trainer. The following is an abbreviated checklist related to this module.

_____Classroom includes a wide variety of appropriate toys and materials. (see pages 24-28)

_____Classroom includes a variety of safe, appropriate, teacher-made toys. (see pages 168-171)

_____Teacher uses projects to provide repeated experiences over time for infants. (see page 28)

_____Teacher plans, implements, and evaluates the success of parent participation activities.

_____Teacher uses Concepts Learned to communicate with parents about their children. (see pages 28-29, 452-463)

_____Teacher identifies resources needed as a part of the planning process.

_____   _____
Teacher Completing Training Module   Date
(please sign and date)

Congratulations! You have completed Module 25 of 38 in the **Teacher's Guide**.

PROP BOXES

Purpose: to learn about prop boxes and make one to use with infants in the classroom

TIME: APPROXIMATELY 1 HOUR

Prop boxes are a way to organize materials that support particular topics in the classroom. Many teachers use copy paper boxes or clear plastic tubs with tops. Label the box (for example, things that go on my head, parents at work, cleaning up, or construction) and plan a place to store prop boxes while they are not in use.

Gather materials to place in the prop box. Check them for safety and ask your mentor or trainer to check the items for safety as well. Plan how to use the prop box in your classroom.

_____   _____

Checked Prop Box Items for Safety   Date

What did you write on the label of the prop box you made?

What materials did you include in the prop box?

How do you plan to use the prop box in the classroom?

Where will you store the prop box when not in use?

Skills Checklist

If you are currently in the classroom, use the complete list on page 95 of this book as a frequent skills checklist to confirm that you are developing your teaching skills repertoire. You may either fill out the skills checklist yourself or ask a teacher to observe you and complete the skills checklist for you (peer evaluation). If you are unfamiliar with an item, read about it in the book or talk with your mentor or trainer. The following is an abbreviated checklist related to this module.

_____Teacher uses projects to provide repeated experiences over time for infants. (see page 28)

_____Teacher plans, implements, and evaluates the success of parent participation activities.

_____Teacher uses Concepts Learned to communicate with parents about their children. (see pages 28-29, 452-463)

_____Teacher identifies resources needed as part of the planning process.

_____Teacher uses prop boxes to gather, organize, and store appropriate materials for use on particular topics in the classroom. (see page 447)

_____   _____

Teacher Completing Training Module   Date
(please sign and date)

Congratulations! You have completed Module 26 of 38 in the **Teacher's Guide**.

PICTURE FILE/VOCABULARY

Purpose: to learn about picture files and vocabulary lists and to begin using both in the classroom

TIME: APPROXIMATELY 1 HOUR

READ THIS

Read the information about picture files/vocabulary on page 29. Also, read some of the lists given for picture files/vocabulary in the Possibilities sections.

Babies are building cognitive images of the things they are experiencing. Pictures help give children a variety of different images, and they also add information to the images that the infants have already experienced.

Begin a picture file by cutting out pictures from magazines, calendars, and posters. Look for pictures that show one image clearly. Trim the edges, attach them to construction paper or cardboard, and laminate or cover them with clear contact paper. Use file folders to sort the pictures by category (for example, families, babies, feet/shoes, hands, faces, furniture, cars, trucks, houses, and so on). Use the pictures to provide cognitive images.

You can add pictures to the environment at children's eye level, attached to the floor to provide images as children scoot or crawl about the environment, or put them together to form simple children's books. Picture files are a source of novelty in the classroom because you can change the photographs from the file to match the topics of Possibilities Plans, to reflect the interests of the children, or to highlight interesting happenings in the larger social world of the child or school.

Picture file pictures also provide acceptance and validation of the diverse images of people who are in our world. Use them to connect children to images from their own culture and ethnic group as well as to diversify the images children have of others. You can also use photographs and pictures as support for emerging literacy skills by pointing out and naming images in the pictures.

You can support infants' vocabulary development as you interact with them throughout the day. Focus on adding words that are new and related to the Possibilities Plans. Write these words in lower case letters with photos, pictures, or illustrations of the word on the page.

Try to use the words frequently in verbal interactions, and in fingerplays and songs with infants.

What picture file/vocabulary categories have you started? List them below. Under each category, list the individual pictures you have collected.

Category _____

            _____

            _____

            _____

            _____

Category _____

            _____

            _____

            _____

            _____

Category _____

            _____

            _____

            _____

            _____

Skills Checklist

If you are currently in the classroom, use the complete list on page 95 of this book as a frequent skills checklist to confirm that you are developing your teaching skills repertoire. You may either fill out the skills checklist yourself or ask a teacher to observe you and complete the skills checklist for you (peer evaluation). If you are unfamiliar with an item, read about it in the book or talk with your mentor or trainer. The following is an abbreviated checklist related to this module.

_____Teacher uses projects to provide repeated experiences over time for infants. (see page 28)

_____Teacher plans, implements, and evaluates the success of parent participation activities.

_____Teacher uses Concepts Learned to communicate with parents about their children. (see pages 28-29, 452-463)

_____Teacher uses prop boxes to gather, organize, and store appropriate materials for use on particular topics in the classroom. (see page 447)

_____Teacher uses picture files and vocabulary to support children's learning about diversity and emerging literacy skills. (see page 29)

_____   _____

Teacher Completing Training Module   Date
(please sign and date)

Congratulations! You have completed Module 27 of 38 in the ***Teacher's Guide***.

BOOKS

Purpose: to explore the importance of books in the classroom, to read to each infant every day, and to create a Books Read List

TIME: APPROXIMATELY 1 HOUR

Reading is a natural part of the early childhood classroom. Through early, positive exposure to reading, children start down the road of literacy development. It is important to read books to each child every day. Keeping a Books Read List communicates to parents what you and the infants are doing during the day and is a part of the documentation of learning in the classroom. Imagine a parent's excitement at seeing the Books Read List beginning to grow and grow, validating that you are spending important one-on-one time with their baby and that you are stimulating the child's emerging interest in the written word.

A form for the Books Read List is in this book on page 109. Each Possibilities section includes suggested books, and often activities in the literacy possibilities are book-related. If you are already in the classroom, begin your own Books Read List and post it in the classroom. Later, you will want to copy the list for each child's portfolio or begin an individual list as the child's interest in particular books emerges. Don't hesitate to put a book on the list more than once! Repetition forms the foundation of interest in more than the pictures—in the words, the direction of reading (left to right), and the story that the words tell on each page.

Where are children's books located in your school?

What is your favorite book for infants?

How do you plan to use it in the classroom?

List some additional ways to get books into your classroom.

Skills Checklist

If you are currently in the classroom, use the complete list on page 95 of this book as a frequent skills checklist to confirm that you are developing your teaching skills repertoire. You may either fill out the skills checklist yourself or ask a teacher to observe you and complete the skills checklist for you (peer evaluation). If you are unfamiliar with an item, read about it in the book or talk with your mentor or trainer. The following is an abbreviated checklist related to this module.

_____Teacher uses projects to provide repeated experiences over time for infants. (see page 28)

_____Teacher plans, implements, and evaluates the success of parent participation activities.

_____Teacher uses Concepts Learned to communicate with parents about their children. (see pages 28-29, 452-463)

_____Teacher uses prop boxes to gather, organize, and store appropriate materials for use on particular topics in the classroom. (see page 447)

_____Teacher uses picture files and vocabulary to support children's learning about diversity and emerging literacy skills. (see page 29)

_____Teacher reads to each child every day. (see page 255)

_____   _____

Teacher Completing Training Module   Date
(please sign and date)

Congratulations! You have completed Module 28 of 38 in the **Teacher's Guide**.

RHYMES/FINGERPLAYS

Purpose: to explore the use of rhymes and fingerplays in the infant classroom, to learn a new rhyme, and to use a new rhyme in the classroom

TIME: APPROXIMATELY 1 HOUR

Rhymes and fingerplays are wonderful ways to support early literacy development for infants. Use them throughout the day as you interact with infants. Read through the section of songs, poems, rhymes, and fingerplays in the appendix (pages 464-468), and choose a new rhyme or fingerplay to learn and use with infants.

READ THIS

Which rhyme/fingerplay did you choose?

How did you use it in the classroom?

What was the child's (children's) reaction during the first exposure?

Will you use the rhyme/fingerplay in a different way the next time you use it? How?

What is the child's (children's) reaction after you have used the fingerplay many times?

Skills Checklist

If you are currently in the classroom, use the complete list on page 95 of this book as a frequent skills checklist to confirm that you are developing your teaching skills repertoire. You may either fill out the skills checklist yourself or ask a teacher to observe you and complete the skills checklist for you (peer evaluation). If you are unfamiliar with an item, read about it in the book or talk with your mentor or trainer. The following is an abbreviated checklist related to this module.

_____Teacher plans, implements, and evaluates the success of parent participation activities.

_____Teacher uses Concepts Learned to communicate with parents about their children. (see pages 28-29, 452-463)

_____Teacher uses prop boxes to gather, organize, and store appropriate materials for use on particular topics in the classroom. (see page 447)

_____Teacher uses picture files and vocabulary to support children's learning about diversity and emerging literacy skills. (see page 29)

_____Teacher reads to each child every day. (see page 255)

_____Teacher uses rhymes/fingerplays while interacting with infants throughout the day. (pages 464-468)

_____   _____

Teacher Completing Training Module   Date
(please sign and date)

Congratulations! You have completed Module 29 of 38 in the **Teacher's Guide**.

MUSIC/SONGS

Purpose: to explore the use of music/songs in the infant classroom, to learn a new song, and to use a new song in the classroom

TIME: APPROXIMATELY 1 HOUR

READ THIS

Music and songs are wonderful ways to support early literacy development for infants. Use them throughout the day as you interact with infants and as you transition from one activity to another. Some research suggests a close link between music experiences and later math abilities. Include music and songs as a natural part of every day. Read through the section on songs, poems, rhymes, and fingerplays in the Appendix (pages 464-468). Choose a new song to learn and use with infants.

Which song did you choose?

How did you use it in the classroom?

What was the child's (children's) reaction to the song?

Will you use the song in a different way next time? How?

Skills Checklist

If you are currently in the classroom, use the complete list on page 95 of this book as a frequent skills checklist to confirm that you are developing your teaching skills repertoire. You may either fill out the skills checklist yourself or ask a teacher to observe you and complete the skills checklist for you (peer evaluation). If you are unfamiliar with an item, read about it in the book or talk with your mentor or trainer. The following is an abbreviated checklist related to this module.

_____Teacher uses prop boxes to gather, organize, and store appropriate materials for use on particular topics in the classroom. (see page 447)

_____Teacher uses picture files and vocabulary to support children's learning about diversity and emerging literacy skills. (see page 29)

_____Teacher reads to each child every day. (see page 255)

_____Teacher uses rhymes/fingerplays while interacting with infants throughout the day. (see pages 464-468)

_____Teacher uses music/songs during the day for interaction and to assist with transitions. (see pages 464-468)

_____   _____

Teacher Completing Training Module   Date
(please sign and date)

Congratulations! You have completed Module 30 of 38 in the **Teacher's Guide**.

TOYS AND MATERIALS (GATHERED AND BOUGHT)

Purpose: to create a storage and sanitation system for toys and materials in the classroom

TIME: APPROXIMATELY 1 HOUR

Read the section "Multiple Sources of Stimulation" on pages 118-120 under Innovations in Environments. Toys and materials are important elements in the infant classroom. Each Possibilities section contains many suggestions for the use of toys and materials, as well as a cumulative list of both gathered and bought materials, to support the activities and experiences contained in the section.

Provide duplicate items since infants do not share. Store toys and materials on low, sturdy shelves in clear, open containers. Bring materials to infants or move infants to where materials are to provide particular experiences. Because infants explore items by mouthing them, you need to have a system for storing and sanitizing toys and materials.

Disinfect items that babies put into their mouths by washing them with soap and water, and then rinsing them in a bleach-and-water solution of ¼ cup bleach to 1 gallon of water. Allow them to air dry. Proper mixing of the bleach water solution is important. Too little bleach will not accomplish the disinfecting; too much bleach is hard on toy surfaces and hands. Keep a measuring cup nearby to make sure you mix the solution correctly. You can also sanitize some toys and materials in a dishwasher. When using an appliance, follow the manufacturer's instructions for adequate sanitation.

Regular sanitation after each use decreases the sharing of colds and other contagious conditions caused by germs containing of surfaces. Many teachers prefer to use a shallow tub in which to place contaminated items until they can be disinfected. (Keep the tub out of the reach of children.) Clearly label containers that have contaminated toys in them to prevent reintroducing them into the classroom before they are sanitized. Always keep bleach in a locked cabinet away from children and bleach solutions out of the reach of children. While disinfecting toys and materials, inspect them for safety. Repair or discard unsafe items immediately.

Find out what the system for the storage and sanitation of toys and materials is at your school, or create a system in your classroom. Describe your system below.

Skills Checklist

If you are currently in the classroom, use the complete list on page 95 of this book as a frequent skills checklist to confirm that you are developing your teaching skills repertoire. You may either fill out the skills checklist yourself or ask a teacher to observe you and complete the skills checklist for you (peer evaluation). If you are unfamiliar with an item, read about it in the book or talk with your mentor or trainer. The following is an abbreviated checklist related to this module.

_____Teacher uses picture files and vocabulary to support children's learning about diversity and emerging literacy skills. (see page 29)

_____Teacher reads to each child every day. (see page 255)

_____Teacher uses rhymes/fingerplays while interacting with infants throughout the day. (see pages 464-468)

_____Teacher uses music/songs during the day for interaction and to assist with transitions. (see pages 464-468)

_____Teacher uses a system for storing and disinfecting toys and materials. (see pages 118-120)

_____   _____

Teacher Completing Training Module   Date
(please sign and date)

Congratulations! You have completed Module 31 of 38 in the **Teacher's Guide**.

USING ANECDOTAL OBSERVATIONS

Purpose: to complete anecdotal observations

TIME: APPROXIMATELY 1 HOUR

Read about anecdotal notes on page 177, "Seeing Children as Unique" on page 19, and "Using Observation and Assessment Strategies" on page 21 in *Innovations: The Comprehensive Infant Curriculum*.

READ THIS

Anecdotal observations of children at play are the foundation of understanding each child's individual developmental pace, unique temperamental traits, and stage of development. Anecdotal observations also serve as a way to uncover play themes and children's emerging interests. You can learn a lot from observing. For example, you might learn when toys and materials lose interest to children or when children need a little less challenge from the environment, toys and materials, and experiences. Additionally, anecdotal observations serve as a record of what is occurring in the classroom (documentation). Finally, observations form the foundation of information to be exchanged with parents during conferences.

Observation is an active process. Good teachers are always observing, and good teachers are always recording their observations to use later as springboards for reflection. *Innovations: The Comprehensive Infant Curriculum* suggests that you observe children regularly and record your observations using Anecdotal Records.

An Anecdotal Record is a specific type of written record of an observation. When making an Anecdotal Record, record only objective information in your observation notes. Focus on what you see, when you see it, how it happens, where the child is, and what is happening. All of these notes are objective. Do not record what you *think* about what you see; just record what is happening.

Then take your observational notes and review them. Look for insight into a child's individual age or stage, ideas about interests and abilities, trends in play, indications that a skill is developing or has developed, and for curriculum ideas that might interest the child.

The following is an example of an anecdotal observation.

Anecdotal Record

Child Ashley Hill   **Date** July 23, 2001   **Time** 9:40a.m.

What I observed Ashley pulled up on the toy shelf and stood. She looked around and then started bouncing up and down by bending her knees. After about two minutes, Ashley sat down and crawled away. A basket of rattles caught her interest. She picked up a red rattle with a round end on it with her left hand. Transferred the rattle to her right hand. Then she put it down. The classroom door opened. Ms. Woods walked in. Ashley watched her for a moment, then began to crawl over to her. As she got close, she sat back on her bottom and looked again. Ms. Woods smiled and Ashley resumed her crawling. When she reached Ms. Woods, she grabbed onto her shirt with two hands and pulled to a stand.

Teacher Miss Tasha

Anecdotal Record

Child   **Date**   **Time**

What I observed

Teacher

Observe three different children. Make three copies of the blank Anecdotal Record and complete one form for each child. Then complete the following tasks for each Anecdotal Record.

Identify the interest the child is showing or demonstrating that you might build a Possibilities Plan around.

Identify which subtask the child is demonstrating or working on.

Identify an emerging developmental domain (such as physical, language, cognitive, and so on) that the child is learning that could be enhanced by a teacher-made toy or a special-directed activity.

Skills Checklist

If you are currently in the classroom, use the complete list on page 95 of this book as a frequent skills checklist to confirm that you are developing your teaching skills repertoire. You may either fill out the skills checklist yourself or ask a teacher to observe you and complete the skills checklist for you (peer evaluation). If you are unfamiliar with an item, read about it in the book or talk with your mentor or trainer. The following is an abbreviated checklist related to this module.

_____Teacher reads to each child every day. (see page 255)
_____Teacher uses picture files and vocabulary to support children's learning about diversity and emerging literacy skills. (see page 29)
_____Teacher uses music/songs during the day for interaction and to assist with transitions. (see pages 464-468)
_____Teacher uses a system for storing and disinfecting toys and materials. (see pages 118-120)
_____Teacher uses anecdotal observations to document learning in the classroom. (see pages 21, 177)

_____   _____
Teacher Completing Training Module   Date
(please sign and date)

Congratulations! You have completed Module 32 of 38 in the **Teacher's Guide**.

PUTTING IT ALL TOGETHER TO PLAN FOR TEACHING

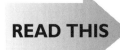

Purpose: to plan for teaching through completing a Possibilities Plan

TIME: APPROXIMATELY 2 HOURS

READ THIS

Read about possibilities planning on pages 445-451. After exploring all the individual elements found in *Innovations: The Comprehensive Infant Curriculum*, you are now prepared to complete an entire Possibilities Plan for your classroom. Choose one of the possibilities sections and begin by reading the web. Use the web as it appears in the book, use a variation of it, or create your own web from scratch. The web will allow you to be flexible in your direction with activities and experiences in the classroom and reflect the children's unique interests and skills.

Copy the blank Possibilities Plan on pages 448-449 or use the one provided on pages 106-107 of this book. Copy your web in the space provided. Use the directions on pages 445-447 and fill in all the sections. Use the sample on pages 450-451 for assistance.

Post the Possibilities Plan in a convenient place in the classroom, so you can refer to it during the day. Parents will enjoy seeing your plan for learning. After you have finished the Possibilities Plan for the infants in your classroom, file it for reference as you develop other plans.

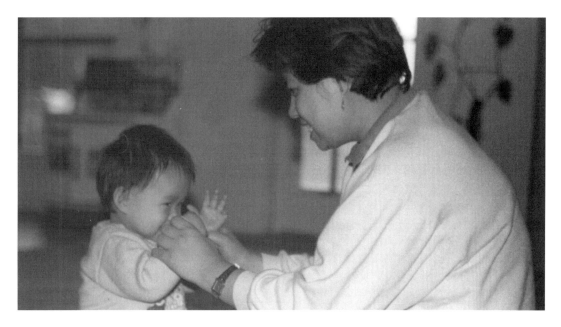

Skills Checklist

If you are currently in the classroom, use the complete list on page 95 of this book as a frequent skills checklist to confirm that you are developing your teaching skills repertoire. You may either fill out the skills checklist yourself or ask a teacher to observe you and complete the skills checklist for you (peer evaluation). If you are unfamiliar with an item, read about it in the book or talk with your mentor or trainer. The following is an abbreviated checklist related to this module.

_____Teacher reads to each child every day. (see page 255)

_____Teacher uses picture files and vocabulary to support children's learning about diversity and emerging literacy skills. (see page 29)

_____Teacher uses music/songs during the day for interaction and to assist with transitions. (see pages 464-468)

_____Teacher uses a system for storing and disinfecting toys and materials. (see pages 118-120)

_____Teacher uses anecdotal observations to document learning in the classroom. (see pages 21, 177)

_____Teacher has complete and appropriate Possibilities Plan posted in the classroom and uses it to provide activities and experiences for infants. (see pages 445-451)

_____   _____

Teacher Completing Training Module   Date
(please sign and date)

Congratulations! You have completed Module 33 of 38 in the **Teacher's Guide**.

MODULE 34

HOW TO USE FORMS TO DOCUMENT CHILDREN'S LEARNING, EVENTS, AND INTERACTIONS

Purpose: to practice using forms to document events, progress, and interactions in the classroom

TIME: APPROXIMATELY 1 HOUR

Documentation of events, progress, and interactions in the classroom is an important part of a teacher's job. Through your experiences thus far in the infant classroom and/or your activities completed as a part of your training, you have already used a number of the forms contained in ***Innovations: The Comprehensive Infant Curriculum***. This training module will give you an opportunity to complete any of the forms you have not yet used. Fill in any of the following blank forms. If you need assistance, refer to the pages listed or talk with your mentor or trainer.

Observation/Assessment Instrument (see pages 19-22, 435-440)
Anecdotal Records (see pages 19-22, 177)
Books Read List (see pages 242-243, 431)
Communication Sheet (see pages 311-312, 429)
Parent Visit Log (see pages 109, 404, 434)
Accident/Incident Form (see pages 183, 432-433)

Skills Checklist

If you are currently in the classroom, use the complete list on page 95 of this book as a frequent skills checklist to confirm that you are developing your teaching skills repertoire. You may either fill out the skills checklist yourself or ask a teacher to observe you and complete the skills checklist for you (peer evaluation). If you are unfamiliar with an item, read about it in the book or talk with your mentor or trainer. The following is an abbreviated checklist related to this module.

_____Teacher uses picture files and vocabulary to support children's learning about diversity and emerging literacy skills. (see page 29)

_____Teacher uses music/songs during the day for interaction and to assist with transitions. (see pages 464-468)

_____Teacher uses a system for storing and disinfecting toys and materials. (see pages 118-120)

_____Teacher uses anecdotal observations to document learning in the classroom. (see pages 21, 177)

_____Teacher has complete and appropriate Possibilities Plan posted in the classroom and uses it to provide activities and experiences for infants. (see pages 445-451)

_____Teacher completes forms to document events, progress, and interactions in the classroom. (see pages 19-22, 109, 177, 183, 242-243, 311-312, 404, 427-440)

_____   _____
Teacher Completing Training Module   Date
(please sign and date)

Congratulations! You have completed Module 34 of 38 in the **_Teacher's Guide_**.

MODULE 35

CONFERENCING WITH PARENTS

Purpose: to learn about conferencing with parents and to have a simulated conference with parents using a variety of materials

TIME: APPROXIMATELY 1 HOUR

READ THIS

Read an explanation of conferencing (pages 375-381). Using the completed developmental assessment on pages 114-121, plan a conference and answer the following questions. Then, simulate conducting an actual conference with parents. Ask your coworkers or your mentor or trainer to role play the part of the parents.

How can you use the assessment to plan a conference with parents?

Write a sentence to show how you can welcome the parent and put him or her at ease.

Write three open-ended questions you can ask based on the results of the assessment.

How can you conclude the conference and make the parent feel comfortable asking questions?

How will you also use anecdotal notes, communication sheets, portfolios, and the Books Read List to make the conference informative and helpful for parents?

Skills Checklist

If you are currently in the classroom, use the complete list on page 95 of this book as a frequent skills checklist to confirm that you are developing your teaching skills repertoire. You may either fill out the skills checklist yourself or ask a teacher to observe you and complete the skills checklist for you (peer evaluation). If you are unfamiliar with an item, read about it in the book or talk with your mentor or trainer. The following is an abbreviated checklist related to this module.

_____Teacher uses music/songs during the day for interaction and to assist with transitions. (see pages 464-468)

_____Teacher uses a system for storing and disinfecting toys and materials. (see pages 118-120)

_____Teacher uses anecdotal observations to document learning in the classroom. (see pages 21, 177)

_____Teacher has complete and appropriate Possibilities Plan posted in the classroom and uses it to provide activities and experiences for infants. (see pages 445-451)

_____Teacher completes forms to document events, progress, and interactions in the classroom. (see pages 19-22, 109, 177, 183, 242-243, 311-312, 404, 427-440)

_____Teacher has periodic conferences with parents using a variety of materials. (see pages 375-381)

_____   _____

Teacher Completing Training Module   Date
(please sign and date)

Congratulations! You have completed Module 35 of 38 in the **Teacher's Guide**.

HOW TO USE PARENT POSTCARDS TO SUPPORT FAMILIES

Purpose: to plan for and use Parent Postcards to support families

TIME: APPROXIMATELY 1 HOUR

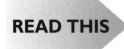

READ THIS

Parent Postcards are an important way to educate parents, establish teachers as the experts in the classroom, and keep parents involved in the education of their children. Read the explanation of postcards as well as the dissemination schedule in the appendix (pages 441-444).

Give out Parent Postcards in chronological order, by topic, or as needs and interests arise. You may give out Parent Postcards more than once. Repetition allows parents to reconsider information or to access it when they "need" to know about the topic.

This section of the curriculum is designed to grow. As you read the professional literature, newspapers, or magazines, look for interesting articles that might appeal to parents. Make copies of these to add to the Parent Postcards. When you find an article of interest, identify when it might be useful to parents and add the title to the dissemination schedule on pages 441-444. That way you will remember to use it again in the future.

You may also choose to write some of your own postcards. For example, you might write a postcard that introduces you to new parents, one that describes your philosophy of early education, or even one that tells parents more about the types of experience you have had in early education. Or, if you have a particular expertise, such as sensory experiences or infant massage, write a postcard to share your special knowledge.

Plan how you will use Parent Postcards for children during the next four weeks. If you are already in the classroom, list the infants in your classroom and plan which postcards will be given out to the parents of each individual child.

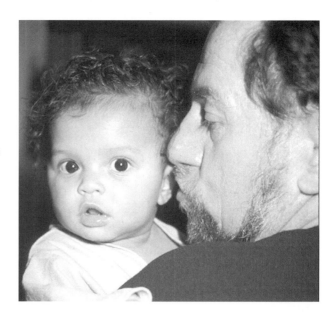

Children's Names	Postcards
Sung Li	Exploratory Biting, page 115

Skills Checklist

If you are currently in the classroom, use the complete list on page 95 of this book as a frequent skills checklist to confirm that you are developing your teaching skills repertoire. You may either fill out the skills checklist yourself or ask a teacher to observe you and complete the skills checklist for you (peer evaluation). If you are unfamiliar with an item, read about it in the book or talk with your mentor or trainer. The following is an abbreviated checklist related to this module.

_____Teacher uses anecdotal observations to document learning in the classroom. (see pages 21, 177)

_____Teacher has complete and appropriate Possibilities Plan posted in the classroom and uses it to provide activities and experiences for infants. (see pages 445-451)

_____Teacher completes forms to document events, progress, and interactions in the classroom. (see pages 19-22, 109, 177, 183, 242-243, 311-312, 404, 427-440)

_____Teacher has periodic conferences with parents using a variety of materials. (see pages 375-381)

_____Teacher plans for and uses Parent Postcards and other resources to support families. (see pages 441-444)

_____   _____
Teacher Completing Training Module   Date
(please sign and date)

Congratulations! You have completed Module 36 of 38 in the *Teacher's Guide*.

MODULE 37

HOW CAN I CONTINUE PROFESSIONAL DEVELOPMENT?

Purpose: to explore ways to continue professional development and to begin a specific plan

TIME: APPROXIMATELY 1 HOUR

The need to grow and learn is a requirement for all individuals, not just children. As an early childhood professional, you will want to continue your professional development so you will continue to grow as a teacher and improve your teaching skills.

The teaching competencies, contained under the Innovations in Teaching section in each chapter, are a great place to start. Start by rating yourself on each item as a self-evaluation. You may also want to ask a colleague or peer to use the list to evaluate your performance in the classroom and recommend areas for further development. Also, use the complete Skills Checklist in this book (pages 95-96) as an evaluation of your emerging skills. Particularly look to see how many of the skills you feel are already in place.

Another source of professional development is to read publications of professional associations. National Association for the Education of Young Children (NAEYC) is the professional association of early childhood educators. It publishes a journal, holds an annual conference, and provides a variety of membership services. Find out if your community has a local or state affiliate of NAEYC and join the association. NAEYC has both a web site (www.naeyc.org) and a toll-free number (800-424-2460).

One of your professional responsibilities is to document all of the formal and informal training in which you participate. Your school may want a record as well to meet licensing or accreditation requirements. You should maintain a current list of all training opportunities in which you participate. Keep copies of brochures announcing the training, training attendance certificates, or registration confirmation as a regular part of your training documentation.

It is also helpful to identify how you will apply the knowledge or information you gain through training opportunities. Reflecting on what you learned and how you will apply it deepens the value of almost any training experience and is part of professional reflective practice.

If you have not already done so, make a plan to pursue further formal training. Begin work towards your CDA or begin course work for an undergraduate or graduate degree. Formal professional development is strongly associated with positive outcomes for children in early childhood programs, so pursuing further professional training is a great way to advance your professional skills while guaranteeing positive outcomes for infants.

Write a paragraph below on how you plan to continue your professional development. Provide specific dates, phone numbers, and goals.

Skills Checklist

If you are currently in the classroom, use the complete list on page 95 of this book as a frequent skills checklist to confirm that you are developing your teaching skills repertoire. You may either fill out the skills checklist yourself or ask a teacher to observe you and complete the skills checklist for you (peer evaluation). If you are unfamiliar with an item, read about it in the book or talk with your mentor or trainer. The following is an abbreviated checklist related to this module.

_____Teacher uses anecdotal observations to document learning in the classroom. (see pages 21, 177)

_____Teacher has complete and appropriate Possibilities Plan posted in the classroom and uses it to provide activities and experiences for infants. (see pages 445-451)

_____Teacher completes forms to document events, progress, and interactions in the classroom. (see pages 19-22, 109, 177, 183, 242-243, 311-312, 404, 427-440)

_____Teacher has periodic conferences with parents using a variety of materials. (see pages 375-381)

_____Teacher plans for and uses Parent Postcards and other resources to support families. (see pages 441-444)

_____Teacher continues growing professionally through reading, training, and professional participation.

_____   _____

Teacher Completing Training Module   Date
(please sign and date)

Congratulations! You have completed Module 37 of 38 in the **Teacher's Guide**.

COMPLETION OF TRAINING

Purpose: to conclude training for *Innovations: The Comprehensive Infant Curriculum*

TIME: APPROXIMATELY 1 HOUR

Today you will complete the final module in your training for *Innovations: The Comprehensive Infant Curriculum*. Begin by reviewing this booklet for any additional questions you might have. Read the pages that are referenced and/or discuss your questions with your mentor or trainer.

After you have completed any questions you might have, look back at Module 3 (page 14 in this book). Review your personal goals for training. Do you have any goals that still need to be achieved? List them below. Use the index to look for additional information on topics you still need to explore.

Ask your mentor or trainer to fill in your Certificate of Completion. Post it in your classroom, so parents can see that you have completed your training for *Innovations: The Comprehensive Infant Curriculum*. Add this training experience to your training records, and place a copy of your certificate of completion in your file.

Skills Checklist

If you are currently in the classroom, use the complete list on page 95 of this book as a frequent skills checklist to confirm that you are developing your teaching skills repertoire. You may either fill out the skills checklist yourself or ask a teacher to observe you and complete the skills checklist for you (peer evaluation). If you are unfamiliar with an item, read about it in the book or talk with your mentor or trainer. The following is an abbreviated checklist related to this module.

_____Teacher uses anecdotal observations to document learning in the classroom. (see pages 21, 177)

_____Teacher has complete and appropriate Possibilities Plan posted in the classroom and uses it to provide activities and experiences for infants. (see pages 445-451)

_____Teacher completes forms to document events, progress, and interactions in the classroom. (see pages 19-22, 109, 177, 183, 242-243, 311-312, 404, 427-440)

_____Teacher plans for and uses Parent Postcards and other resources to support families. (see pages 441-444)

_____Teacher continues growing professionally through reading, training, and other methods.

_____Teacher has copies of the Completion of Training, as well as other credentials, documented and/or posted in the classroom.

_____   _____
Teacher Completing Training Module   Date
(please sign and date)

Congratulations! You have completed Module 38 of 38 in the **_Teacher's Guide_**.

INNOVATIONS:

COMPLETION OF **41 HOURS** OF TRAINING IN

The Comprehensive Infant Curriculum

NAME

SCHOOL

DATE

MENTOR or TRAINER

Use this Skills Checklist for self evaluation, peer evaluation by another teacher, or performance evaluation by your supervisor/director.

_____ _____

Teacher Name   Date

_____Parents and infants are greeted warmly. (see pages 35-36)

_____Toys and equipment are disinfected. (see page 119)

_____Diapering procedures are followed. (see pages 310-311)

_____Quality interactions occur during the day. (see page 233)

_____Safety precautions are followed in the classroom (for example, attendance taken, infants never left alone, chokeable items eliminated, toys and materials regularly checked for safety). (see page 307)

_____Teacher observes infants regularly during the day. (see pages 19-21)

_____Assessment materials are readily available in the classroom (clipboard, pen, forms). (see pages 21-22)

_____Teacher explores and discovers the relationship between behavior and child development principles. (see page 34)

_____Teacher uses routine times to provide individual quality interactions for infants. (see pages 35-36)

_____Teacher uses reflection to assess and improve teaching competencies. (see page 23)

_____Teacher supports partnerships with parents through planning and implementing regular parent participation opportunities. (see page 23)

_____Teacher modifies parent participation choices as a result of reflection about the success of planned activities.

_____Teacher creates, maintains, and refreshes appropriate classroom environment. (see pages 55-57)

_____Classroom contains experiences and activities that reflect a wide variety of possibilities for children in the classroom. (see pages 24-28)

_____Teacher uses webbing as a technique to support emergent curriculum. (see page 24)

_____Classroom includes a wide variety of appropriate toys and materials. (see pages 24-29)

_____Classroom includes a variety of safe, appropriate, teacher-made toys. (see pages 168-171)

_____Teacher uses projects to provide repeated experiences over time for infants. (see page 28)

_____Teacher plans, implements, and evaluates the success of parent participation activities.

_____Teacher uses Concepts Learned to communicate with parents about their children. (see pages 28-29, 452-463)

_____Teacher identifies resources needed as a part of the planning process.

_____Teacher uses prop boxes to gather, organize, and store appropriate materials for use on particular topics in the classroom. (see page 447)

_____Teacher uses picture files and vocabulary to support children's learning about diversity and emerging literacy skills. (see page 29)

_____Teacher reads to each child every day. (see page 255)

_____Teacher uses rhymes/fingerplays while interacting with infants throughout the day. (pages 464-468)

_____Teacher uses music/songs during the day for interaction and to assist with transitions. (see pages 464-468)

_____Teacher uses a system for storing and disinfecting toys and materials. (see pages 118-120)

_____Teacher uses anecdotal observations to document learning in the classroom. (see pages 21, 177)

_____Teacher has complete and appropriate Possibilities Plan posted in the classroom and uses it to provide activities and experiences for infants. (see pages 445-451)

_____Teacher completes forms to document events, progress, and interactions in the classroom. (see pages 19-22, 109, 177, 183, 242-243, 311-312, 404, 427-440)

_____Teacher has periodic conferences with parents using a variety of materials. (see pages 375-381)

_____Teacher plans for and uses Parent Postcards and other resources to support families. (see pages 441-444)

_____Teacher continues growing professionally through reading, training, and professional participation.

_____Teacher has copies of the Completion of Training, as well as other credentials, documented and/or posted in the classroom.

Innovations: The Comprehensive Infant Curriculum

Observation/Assessment
Birth to 18 months

Observation/Assessment

CHILD'S NAME   TEACHER

Infant (0-18 months) Assessment

Task: *Separating from Parents*

	0-6 months	6-12 months		12-18 months
S1	a. Little or no experience with separating from Mom and Dad; accepts sensitive care from substitute.	b. Some experience with separating from Mom and Dad; prefers familiar caregiver, but accepts sensitive care from substitute.	c. More experience with separating from Mom and Dad; resists separating; shows distress upon separation, and takes time to adjust.	d. Experienced with separating from Mom and Dad; resists initial separation, but adjusts after only a few moments.
S2	a. Startled by new sounds, smells, and people.	b. Orients toward new or interesting stimuli.		c. Seeks new and interesting stimuli.
S3	a. Accepts transitions without notice.	b. Reacts with discomfort during the transition.	c. Resists transition preparation as well as the transition.	d. Anticipates transitions when preparation activities begin. If preparation is to a preferred, familiar activity, transition is accepted.
S4	a. Displays indiscriminate attachment; will accept sensitive care from most familiar adults; exhibits preference for Mom, Dad, or familiar caregiver if present.	b. Displays discriminate attachment; will still accept care from sensitive caregivers, but prefers care from Mom, Dad, or familiar caregivers.		c. Separation anxiety emerges; resists approaches by unfamiliar adults and resists separation from Mom, Dad, and familiar caregivers. Cries, clings, calls for parents when they leave the child's view.
S5	a. Unpredictable daily schedule.	b. Patterns in daily schedule emerge around eating and sleeping.		c. Daily schedule is predictable. Eating and sleeping patterns are relatively stable and predictable.
S6	a. Feeds from breast or bottle.	b. Begins to take baby food from a spoon; begins to sip from a cup.		c. Drinks from bottle and/or cup; eats finger foods.
S7	a. Plays with objects within visual field; bats at objects with hands and feet.	b. Manipulates, mouths, and plays with objects; likes action/reaction toys. Plays with objects then drops them to move on to new objects. May return to objects again and again.		c. Plays with favorite things again and again. Likes to dump out objects and play with them on the floor. Considers all objects and toys in the environment personal play choices, even when being played with by others.

Infant (0-18 months) Assessment

Task: Connecting with School and Teacher

	0-6 months		6-12 months	12-18 months
C1	a. Does not resist separating from parents.		b. Resists separating from parents; resists comfort from primary teacher.	c. Resists separating from parents; accepts comfort from primary teacher.
C2	a. Accepts transition from parent to teacher.		b. Maintains physical proximity to primary teacher during separation.	c. Seeks primary teacher's support in separating.
C3	a. Comforts after a period of distress.		b. Comforts quickly after being picked up.	c. Comforts when needs or wants are acknowledged by caregiver.
C4	a. Is unaware of friends in classroom.		b. Visually notices friends in classroom.	c. Gets excited about seeing friends; seeks physical proximity.
C5	a. Uses parents and teacher physically to support exploration of the environment; explores objects placed nearby parents and teachers.		b. Uses parents and teacher visually to support exploration of the environment; manipulates objects found in environment.	c. Explores the environment independently; responds to play cues presented by adults.
C6	a. Focuses on face-to-face interaction.	b. Tracks moving object up and down and right to left.	c. Watches people, objects, and activities in immediate environment.	d. Initiates interactions with people, toys, and the environment.
C7	a. Objects exist only when in view.	b. Objects perceived as having separate existence.	c. Looks where objects were last seen after they disappear.	d. Follows visual displacement of objects.
C8	a. Thinks object disappears when it moves out of view.	b. Looks where object was last seen after it disappears.	c. Follows object as it disappears.	d. Searches for hidden object if the disappearance was observed.

Infant (0-18 months) Assessment

Task: Relating to Self and Others

	0-6 months	6-12 months		12-18 months
R1	a. Calms self with adult support.	b. Calms self with support from adults and/or transitional objects.		c. Calms self with transitional objects.
R2	a. Unaware of own image in mirror.	b. Curious about own image in mirrors and photographs.	c. Discovers self in mirror and photographs.	d. Differentiates own image from images of others.
R3	a. Begins to demonstrate preferences for different types of sensory stimuli.	b. Prefers some types of stimuli to others.		c. Is interested in pursuing favorite stimulation activities again and again.
R4	a. Develops a multi-sensory interest in the world—wants to see, touch, mouth, hear, and hold objects.	b. Uses senses to explore and discover the near environment.		c. Uses motor movements to enhance sensory exploration of the environment.
R5	a. Play is predominantly unoccupied in nature.	b. Play is predominantly onlooker in nature.	c. Play is predominantly solitary in nature.	
R6	a. Exhibits practice play.			b. Exhibits symbolic play.
R7	a. Develops an interest in the human world.	b. Seeks interactions with responsive adults; interested also in what other children are doing.	c. Seeks most interactions with familiar adults; fascinated by what other children are doing.	d. Prefers interactions with familiar adults; resists interaction with unfamiliar adults; may be cautious with unfamiliar friends.
R8	a. Does not distinguish between needs (social interaction, a new position, holding instead of lying in the bed) and wants (food, diaper changes, sleep).	b. Begins to distinguish between needs and wants; can communicate differently about different needs and wants.	c. Uses objects, gestures, and behaviors to indicate needs and wants.	d. Uses single words to indicate needs and wants like "muk" for "I want milk," or "bye-bye" for "Let's go bye-bye."
R9	a. Creates mental images of emotions and emotional responses to situations.			b. Begins to understand how feelings relate to others.
R10	a. Unable to negotiate interactions with peers without direct adult support and facilitation.	b. Calls for help loudly by crying or screaming when problems occur during exploration of the environment or with peers.	c. Exchanges or trades with peers to get a desired toy or material with direct adult support and facilitation.	d. Asks other children to walk away when conflict arises between children; expects the other child to do so.
R11	a. Explores environment and the things in it orally. May bite, poke, scratch, or pinch others during exploration.			b. Experiments with behavior that gets a reaction; may bite, pinch, poke, scratch during interactions with others to see what happens.

Infant (0-18 months) Assessment

Task: Communicating with Parents, Teachers, and Friends

	0-6 months			6-12 months		12-18 months
CM1	a. Gazes at familiar faces.	b. Responds to facial expressions of familiar faces.	c. Occasionally engages in reciprocal communication with facial expressions, vowel sounds, and voice inflection.	d. Frequently engages in reciprocal communication using facial expressions, inflection, and vowel and consonant sounds.		e. Imitates and jabbers in response to familiar voices.
CM2	a. Makes sounds.	b. Imitiates intonational and inflectional vocal patterns.		c. Develops holophrasic speech—words that convey complete sentences or thoughts.	d. Uses the same word to convey different meaning.	e. Develops telegraphic speech, where 2 or 3 words are used as a sentence.
CM3	a. Listens to familiar people's voices when they talk.	b. Shows understanding of simple phrases by responding or reacting.		c. Points to or looks at familiar objects when asked to do so.		d. Follows commands with visual cues or context cues.
CM4	a. Babbles motorically, acoustically, and visually simple sounds like (m), (p), (b), (n) at the beginning of words and vowel sounds like (ah), (oh), (uh).			b. Babbles sounds like (w), (k), (f), (t), (d) at the beginning of words and vowels sounds like (eh), (ee); strings sounds together (ba-ba-ba-ba-ba) and practices sounds in a wide variety of ways.		
CM5	a. Responds discriminantly to voices of mother and father.	b. Turns toward and responds to familiar voices and sounds.		c. Prefers familiar sounds and voices.		d. Directs vocalizations toward familiar people and objects in the environment.
CM6	a. Experiments with babbling and cooing.	b. Inflection is added to babbling and cooing.				c. Single words or phrases are understandable to familiar adults; strangers may not understand these words.
CM7	a. Looks at picture books.	b. Listens to books when read by a familiar adult.			c. Points to pictures.	d. Turns pages.

Infant (0-18 months) Assessment

Task: Moving Around Home and School

	0-6 months	6-12 months	12-18 months
M1	a. Holds head away from shoulder. b. Holds head steady side to side. c. Holds head up when lying on stomach. d. Rolls from back to front. e. Rolls from front to back.	f. Scoots on stomach. g. Sits with support. h. Sits without support. i. Crawls after ball or toy. j. Pulls to a stand.	k. Lowers back down to squatting position. l. Walks with support. m. Walks without support. n. Squats down and stands back up. o. Climbs into chair. p. Kicks ball.
M2	a. Eyes and head follow motion. b. Holds rattle. c. Exchanges objects between hands.	d. Uses pincher grasp to pick up small items. e. Picks up toys and objects. f. Dumps objects out of containers. g. Puts objects back into containers. h. Scribbles.	i. Turns pages in cardboard book. j. Unbuttons large buttons. k. Completes puzzles with 2-3 pieces.

Infant (0-18 months) Assessment

Task: Expressing Feelings with Parents, Teachers, and Friends

	0-6 months	6-12 months	12-18 months
E1	a. Begins to self-regulate; calms self after sensitive response from a caring adult.	b. Expects adults to respond to social cues such as vocalization, gestures, or cries.	c. Knows which behaviors will make caregivers react in certain ways (for example, which actions will make you laugh and which ones will make you say "stop").
E2	a. Develops an interest in the world; is alert to sounds, touch, and faces.	b. Explores the environment; picks up objects of interest, then moves on to other objects.	c. Plays in a focused, organized manner.
E3	a. Gazes at faces with interest; smiles responsively.	b. Reaches up to indicate an interest in being held; is interested in social interaction with familiar adults.	c. Uses physical behavior (such as crawling over and pulling up) to establish closeness to caregivers.
E4	a. Seeks interactions with familiar people; vocalizes in response to vocalization.	b. Seeks to explore interesting toys, objects, and people.	c. Responds to limits that are set verbally; complies only with support from adults.
E5	a. Emotional reactions continue for a minute or two after an adult responds; does not recognize the change in state immediately.	b. Begins to coordinate behavior and emotions by acting on feelings; connects physical actions with needs (for example, goes over to the refrigerator to indicate interest in food or drink).	c. Recovers from emotional outbursts in a few minutes most of the time.

	0-6 months		6-12 months		12-18 months	
	Subtask	Date	Subtask	Date	Subtask	Date
Task 1 Separating from Parents	S1a		S1b		S1d	
			S1c			
	S2a		S2b		S2c	
	S3a		S3b		S3d	
			S3c			
	S4a		S4b		S4c	
	S5a		S5b		S5c	
	S6a		S6b		S6c	
	S7a		S7b		S7c	
Task 2 Connecting with School and Teacher	C1a		C1b		C1c	
	C2a		C2b		C2c	
	C3a		C3b		C3c	
	C4a		C4b		C4c	
	C5a		C5b		C5c	
	C6a		C6c		C6d	
	C6b					
	C7a		C7c		C7d	
	C7b					
	C8a		C8c		C8d	
	C8b					
Task 3 Relating to Self and Others	R1a		R1b		R1c	
	R2a		R2b		R2d	
			R2c			
	R3a		R3b		R3c	
	R4a		R4b		R4c	
	R5a		R5b		R5c	
			R5c			
	R6a		R6a		R6b	
	R7a		R7b		R7d	
			R7c			
	R8a		R8b		R8d	
			R8c			
	R9a		R9a		R9b	
	R10a		R10b		R10d	
			R10c			
	R11a		R11a		R11b	

	0-6 months		6-12 months		12-18 months	
	Subtask	Date	Subtask	Date	Subtask	Date
Task 4 **Communicating** **with Parents,** **Teachers, and Friends**	CM1a		CM1d		CM1e	
	CM1b					
	CM1c					
	CM2a		CM2c		CM2e	
	CM2b		CM2d			
	CM3a		CM3c		CM3d	
	CM3b					
	CM4a		CM4b		CM4b	
	CM5a		CM5c		CM5d	
	CM5b					
	CM6a		CM6b		CM6c	
	CM6b					
	CM7a		CM7b		CM7c	
	CM7b				CM7d	
Task 5 **Moving around** **Home and School**	M1a		M1f		M1k	
	M1b		M1g		M1l	
	M1c		M1h		M1m	
	M1d		M1i		M1n	
	M1e		M1j		M1o	
					M1p	
	M2a		M2e		M2i	
	M2b		M2f		M2j	
	M2c		M2g		M2k	
	M2d		M2h			
Task 6 **Expressing Feelings** **with Parents,** **Teachers, and Friends**	E1a		E1b		E1c	
	E2a		E2b		E2c	
	E3a		E3b		E3c	
	E4a		E4b		E4c	
	E5a		E5b		E5c	

Possibilities

Parent Possibilities

Teacher-Initiated

Parent Participation

Innovations in Environments

Observation/Assessment Possibilities

Interactive Experiences

Plan

Web

Dramatic Possibilities

Art/Sensory Possibilities

Curiosity Possibilities

Music Possibilities

Movement Possibilities

Literacy Possibilities

Outdoor Possibilities

Project Possibilities

Books

Picture File Pictures/Vocabulary

Rhymes & Fingerplays

Music/Songs

Prop Boxes

INNOVATIONS

Anecdotal Record

Child Date Time

What I observed

Teacher

INNOVATIONS

Anecdotal Record

Child Date Time

What I observed

Teacher

Books Read List

Book Title	Date
1.	
2.	
3.	
4.	
5.	
6.	
7.	
8.	
9.	
10.	
11.	
12.	
13.	
14.	
15.	
16.	
17.	
18.	
19.	
20.	
21.	
22.	
23.	
24.	
25.	
26.	
27.	
28.	
29.	
30.	

Communication Sheet

CHILD'S NAME

FOR THE WEEK OF

DAY	BREAKFAST	TOTAL HOURS SLEPT	BEHAVIOR CHANGES NOTICED	PARENT COMMENTS/INSTRUCTIONS	FOODS EATEN SOLIDS	FOODS EATEN LIQUIDS	DIAPER CHANGES		NAPTIME START	NAPTIME WOKE	TEACHER COMMENTS
M	YES / NO		YES / NO				WET	BM			
T	YES / NO		YES / NO				WET	BM			
W	YES / NO		YES / NO				WET	BM			
Th	YES / NO		YES / NO				WET	BM			
F	YES / NO		YES / NO				WET	BM			

Parent Visit Log

School Name _____

Date	Name of Parent
1. _____	
2. _____	
3. _____	
4. _____	
5. _____	
6. _____	
7. _____	
8. _____	
9. _____	
10. _____	
11. _____	
12. _____	
13. _____	
14. _____	
15. _____	
16. _____	
17. _____	
18. _____	
19. _____	
20. _____	
21. _____	
22. _____	
23. _____	
24. _____	
25. _____	
26. _____	
27. _____	
28. _____	
29. _____	
30. _____	

Accident/Incident Report
(for school records)

Name of injured child

Date of accident/incident

Location of accident (address)

Site (place in school)

What happened? Describe what took place.

Why did it happen? Give all of the facts—why? where? what? when? who? etc.

What should be done to prevent this accident from recurring?

If the accident involved a child, how were the parents notified and by whom?

What was the parent's reaction?

What has been done so far to correct the situation?

With whom was this accident discussed, other than the child's parents?

Reported by   Date

HELPFUL HINTS FOR COMPLETING OBSERVATIONS AND ASSESSMENTS

Plan to observe regularly, but don't overlook daily observations that occur in real time. If you note a new skill or play interest, write it on the Communication Sheet so you won't forget it and attach a copy of the Communication Sheet to the assessment. Use these "real time" observations to support formal observations.

Take anecdotal notes as you observe. Notes can be about one child, or about more than one child. If you record information about more than one child, copy the note and file it in both children's files.

After taking anecdotal notes, look at the appropriate assessment to determine if you observed any of the assessment items listed. If you did, simply date the assessment item, indicating that you have an anecdotal note that documents your observation of the skill (i.e., Anecdotal Note, 3/3/00).

Put the date ranges for the child on the chart below the age ranges to cue you to the child's birthdate and confirm you are observing the right sections.

Look for secondary sources for some assessment items. For example, check Communication Sheets, Books Read Lists, word lists, anecdotal notes, and any other sources of information to see if you can confirm the presence of skills from these sources.

If you don't observe an item during the time range of the skill, and subsequent skills are noted, put "not observed (N/O)" in the date space.

Completed Developmental Assessment

Infant (0-18 months) Assessment

Task: Separating from Parents

	0-6 months 7/13/98 – 1/13/99	6-12 months 1/13/99 – 7/13/99		12-18 months 7/13/99 – 1/13/00
S1	a. Little or no experience with separating from Mom and Dad; accepts sensitive care from substitute. 8/30/98: takes bottle from teacher	b. Some experience with separating from Mom and Dad; prefers familiar caregiver, but accepts sensitive care from substitute. See AN 10/1/98	c. More experience with separating from Mom and Dad; resists separating; shows distress upon separation, and takes time to adjust. 4/1/99	d. Experienced with separating from Mom and Dad; resists initial separation, but adjusts after only a few moments. AN: 8/16/99
S2	a. Startled by new sounds, smells, and people. 9/2/98: Door slams, Abby's cry	b. Orients toward new or interesting stimuli. 9/15/98: B&W mobile over changing table		c. Seeks new and interesting stimuli. 6/30/99
S3	a. Accepts transitions without notice. 8/13/98: Accepted transition from mom to teacher	b. Reacts with discomfort during the transition. N/O	c. Resists transition preparation as well as the transition. N/O	d. Anticipates transitions when preparation activities begin. If preparation is to a preferred, familiar activity, transition is accepted. 11/15/99
S4	a. Displays indiscriminate attachment; will accept sensitive care from most familiar adults; exhibits preference for Mom, Dad, or familiar caregiver if present. 8/30/98	b. Displays discriminate attachment; will still accept care from sensitive caregivers, but prefers care from Mom, Dad, or familiar caregivers. 3/1/99 Likes Gwynethia when Louisa at lunch		c. Separation anxiety emerges; resists approaches by unfamiliar adults and resists separation from Mom, Dad, and familiar caregivers. Cries, clings, calls for parents when they leave the child's view. 7/15/99 See com. sheet 7/15/99
S5	a. Unpredictable daily schedule. 8/30/98 See Daily Schedule Form, child file	b. Patterns in daily schedule emerge around eating and sleeping. See AN 11/30/98 See Daily Schedule Form		c. Daily schedule is predictable. Eating and sleeping patterns are relatively stable and predictable. 9/1/99
S6	a. Feeds from breast or bottle. breast milk in bottle 8/30/98	b. Begins to take baby food from a spoon; begins to sip from a cup. spoon 3/15/99 cup 7/5/99		c. Drinks from bottle and/or cup; eats finger foods. Cup only 10/10/99 finger foods 7/15/99 (AN)
S7	a. Plays with objects within visual field; bats at objects with hands and feet. 10/23/98	b. Manipulates, mouths, and plays with objects; likes action/reaction toys. Plays with objects then drops them to move on to new objects. May return to objects again and again. 2/14/99		c. Plays with favorite things again and again. Likes to dump out objects and play with them on the floor. Considers all objects and toys in the environment personal play choices, even when being played with by others. 10/30/99

Infant (0-18 months) Assessment

Task: Connecting with School and Teacher

	0-6 months 7/13/98 – 1/13/99		6-12 months 1/13/99 – 7/13/99	12-18 months 7/13/99 – 1/13/00
C1	a. Does not resist separating from parents. 8/31/98		b. Resists separating from parents; resists comfort from primary teacher. 4/1/99	c. Resists separating from parents; accepts comfort from primary teacher. AN 8/16/99
C2	a. Accepts transition from parent to teacher. N/O		b. Maintains physical proximity to primary teacher during separation. 4/1/99	c. Seeks primary teacher's support in separating. AN 8/16/99
C3	a. Comforts after a period of distress. AN 8/30/98		b. Comforts quickly after being picked up. AN 12/6/98	c. Comforts when needs or wants are acknowledged by caregiver. AN 8/16/99
C4	a. Is unaware of friends in classroom. 9/2/98		b. Visually notices friends in classroom. 2/15/99	c. Gets excited about seeing friends; seeks physical proximity. 11/3/99
C5	a. Uses parents and teacher physically to support exploration of the environment; explores objects placed nearby parents and teachers. AN 12/6/98		b. Uses parents and teacher visually to support exploration of the environment; manipulates objects found in environment. AN 3/28/99	c. Explores the environment independently; responds to play cues presented by adults. 5/2/99
C6	a. Focuses on face-to-face interaction. 8/30/98	b. Tracks moving object up and down and right to left. 10/1/98	c. Watches people, objects, and activities in immediate environment. 1/31/99	d. Initiates interactions with people, toys, and the environment. 6/1/99
C7	a. Objects exist only when in view. 8/30/98	b. Objects perceived as having separate existence. AN 10/1/98	c. Looks where objects were last seen after they disappear. Looked for cup on table after it fell on floor 1/31/99	d. Follows visual displacement of objects. Played "Where's the Kitty?" followed 3 displacements visually 8/15/99
C8	a. Thinks object disappears when it moves out of view. 9/2/98	b. Looks where object was last seen after it disappears. AN 11/30/98	c. Follows object as it disappears. AN 3/28/99	d. Searches for hidden object if the disappearance was observed. Pulled blanket off of teddy after hiding it 8/15/99

Infant (0-18 months) Assessment

Task: Relating to Self and Others

	0-6 months 7/13/98 – 1/13/99	6-12 months 1/13/99 – 7/13/99		12-18 months 7/13/99 – 1/13/00
R1	a. Calms self with adult support. 8/30/98	b. Calms self with support from adults and/or transitional objects. Likes silky blanket 1/16/99		c. Calms self with transitional objects.
R2	a. Unaware of own image in mirror. N/O	b. Curious about own image in mirrors and photographs. N/O	c. Discovers self in mirror and photographs. AN 3/16/99	d. Differentiates own image from images of others.
R3	a. Begins to demonstrate preferences for different types of sensory stimuli. AN 10/1/98	b. Prefers some types of stimuli to others. 11/13/99 Loves books, action/reaction toys, push/pull toys and stuffed animals		c. Is interested in pursuing favorite stimulation activities again and again. 5/1/99 Stroller rides!
R4	a. Develops a multi-sensory interest in the world—wants to see, touch, mouth, hear, and hold objects. 9/2/98	b. Uses senses to explore and discover the near environment. 3/28/99		c. Uses motor movements to enhance sensory exploration of the environment. 4/28/99
R5	a. Play is predominantly unoccupied in nature. 9/2/98	b. Play is predominantly onlooker in nature. 1/30/99	c. Play is predominantly 6/1/99 solitary in nature.	
R6	a. Exhibits practice play. AN 3/16/99 AN 8/16/99			b. Exhibits symbolic play.
R7	a. Develops an interest in the human world. Gazes at teacher's face 9/2/98	b. Seeks interactions with responsive adults; interested also in what other children are doing. 1/31/99	c. Seeks most interactions with familiar adults; fascinated by what other children are doing. 2/14/99	d. Prefers interactions with familiar adults; resists interaction with unfamiliar adults; may be cautious with unfamiliar friends.
R8	a. Does not distinguish between needs (social interaction, a new position, holding instead of lying in the bed) and wants (food, diaper changes, sleep). 8/30/98	b. Begins to distinguish between needs and wants; can communicate differently about different needs and wants. 2/14/99	c. Uses objects, gestures, and behaviors to indicate needs and wants. Points and says "meomeomeo" means "milk" 2/15/99	d. Uses single words to indicate needs and wants like "muk" for "I want milk," or "bye-bye" for "Let's go bye-bye."
R9	a. Creates mental images of emotions and emotional responses to situations. AN 11/30/98 AN 12/6/98			b. Begins to understand how feelings relate to others.
R10	a. Unable to negotiate interactions with peers without direct adult support and facilitation. 8/30/98	b. Calls for help loudly by crying or screaming when problems occur during exploration of the environment or with peers. AN 12/6/98	c. Exchanges or trades with peers to get a desired toy or material with direct adult support and facilitation.	d. Asks other children to walk away when conflict arises between children; expects the other child to do so.
R11	a. Explores environment and the things in it orally. May bite, poke, scratch, or pinch others during exploration. AN 11/30/98 AN 12/6/98 AN 8/16/99			b. Experiments with behavior that gets a reaction; may bite, pinch, poke, scratch during interactions with others to see what happens.

Infant (0-18 months) Assessment

Task: Communicating with Parents, Teachers, and Friends

	0-6 months 7/13/98 – 1/13/99			6-12 months 1/13/99 – 7/13/99		12-18 months 7/13/99 – 1/13/00	
CM1	a. Gazes at familiar faces. 8/30/98	b. Responds to facial expressions of familiar faces. 8/30/98	c. Occasionally engages in reciprocal communication with facial expressions, vowel sounds, and voice inflection. 10/31/98	d. Frequently engages in reciprocal communication using facial expressions, inflection, and vowel and consonant sounds. 11/15/98		e. Imitates and jabbers in response to familiar voices. 2/15/99	
CM2	a. Makes sounds. 8/30/98	b. Imitiates intonational and inflectional vocal patterns. 11/30/98		c. Develops holophrasic speech—words that convey complete sentences or thoughts. 12/15/98	d. Uses the same word to convey different meaning. meomeomeo means milk, juice, water 1/4/99	e. Develops telegraphic speech, where 2 or 3 words are used as a sentence.	
CM3	a. Listens to familiar people's voices when they talk. 9/2/98	b. Shows understanding of simple phrases by responding or reacting. 12/15/98		c. Points or looks at familiar objects when asked to do so. 2/14/99		d. Follows commands with visual cues or context cues. Goes to door when teacher says it's time to go outside 5/1/99	
CM4	a. Babbles motorically, acoustically, and visually simple sounds like (m), (p), (b), (n) at the beginning of words and vowel sounds like (ah), (oh), (uh). See		sound list in file	b. Babbles sounds like (w), (k), (f), (t), (d) at the beginning of words and vowels sounds like (eh), (ee); strings sounds together (ba-ba-ba-ba-ba) and practices sounds in a wide variety of ways.			
CM5	a. Responds discriminantly to voices of mother and father. 8/31/98	b. Turns toward and responds to familiar voices and sounds. 1/13/99		c. Prefers familiar sounds and voices. 2/15/99		d. Directs vocalizations toward familiar people and objects in the environment. 4/1/99	
CM6	a. Experiments with babbling and cooing. 2/15/99	b. Inflection is added to babbling and cooing. AN 3/1/99				c. Single words or phrases are understandable to familiar adults; strangers may not understand these words. See word list in file	
CM7	a. Looks at picture books. 1/30/99	b. Listens to books when read by a familiar adult. 2/14/99				c. Points to pictures. 2/14/99	d. Turns pages. 5/14/99

Infant (0-18 months) Assessment

Task: Moving Around Home and School

M1

0-6 months (7/13/98 – 1/13/99)

	Skill	Date
a.	Holds head away from shoulder.	8/30/98 8/30/98
b.	Holds head steady side to side.	8/30/98
c.	Holds head up when lying on stomach.	9/5/98
d.	Rolls from back to front.	11/98
e.	Rolls from front to back.	11/19/98

6-12 months (1/13/99 – 7/13/99)

	Skill	Date
f.	Scoots on stomach.	2/15/99
g.	Sits with support.	4/1/99
h.	Sits without support.	5/1/99
i.	Crawls after ball or toy.	6/1/99
j.	Pulls to a stand.	6/1/99

12-18 months (7/13/99 – 1/13/00)

	Skill	Date
k.	Lowers back down to squatting position.	6/1/99
l.	Walks with support.	8/2/99
m.	Walks without support.	10/1/99
n.	Squats down and stands back up.	11/5/99
o.	Climbs into chair.	1/1/00
p.	Kicks ball.	

M2

0-6 months (7/13/98 – 1/13/99)

	Skill	Date
a.	Eyes and head follow motion.	8/30/98
b.	Holds rattle.	10/1/98
c.	Exchanges objects between hands.	12/23/98
d.	Uses pincher grasp to pick up small items.	1/29/99

6-12 months (1/13/99 – 7/13/99)

	Skill	Date
e.	Picks up toys and objects.	12/23/98
f.	Dumps objects out of containers.	4/1/99
g.	Puts objects back into containers.	5/1/99
h.	Scribbles.	8/4/99

12-18 months (7/13/99 – 1/13/00)

	Skill	Date
i.	Turns pages in cardboard book.	5/4/99
j.	Unbuttons large buttons.	12/17/99
k.	Completes puzzles with 2-3 pieces.	

Infant (0-18 months) Assessment

Task: Expressing Feelings with Parents, Teachers, and Friends

	0-6 months 7/13/98 – 1/13/99	**6-12 months** 1/13/99 – 7/13/99	**12-18 months** 7/13/99 – 1/13/00
E1	a. Begins to self-regulate; calms self after sensitive response from a caring adult. 8/30/98	b. Expects adults to respond to social cues such as vocalization, gestures, or cries	c. Knows which behaviors will make caregivers react in certain ways (for example, which actions will make you laugh and which ones will make you say "stop").
E2	a. Develops an interest in the world; is alert to sounds, touch, and faces. 9/2/98	b. Explores the environment; picks up objects of interest, then moves on to other objects. 4/1/99	c. Plays in a focused, organized manner.
E3	a. Gazes at faces with interest; smiles responsively. 8/30/98	b. Reaches up to indicate an interest in being held; is interested in social interaction with familiar adults. AN 3/2/99	c. Uses physical behavior (such as crawling over and pulling up) to establish closeness to caregivers. 7/15/99
E4	a. Seeks interactions with familiar people; vocalizes in response to vocalization. 9/2/98	b. Seeks to explore interesting toys, objects, and people. 1/31/99	c. Responds to limits that are set verbally; complies only with support from adults.
E5	a. Emotional reactions continue for a minute or two after an adult responds; does not recognize the change in state immediately. 8/30/98	b. Begins to coordinate behavior and emotions by acting on feelings; connects physical actions with needs (for example, goes over to the refrigerator to indicate interest in food or drink). 2/15/99	c. Recovers from emotional outbursts in a few minutes most of the time.

Infant (0-18 months) Observation and Assessment Summary

	0-6 months		6-12 months		12-18 months	
	Subtask	Date	Subtask	Date	Subtask	Date
Task 1 **Separating from** **Parents**	S1a	8/30/98	S1b	10/1/98	S1d	8/16/99
			S1c	4/1/99		
	S2a	9/2/98	S2b	9/15/98	S2c	6/30/99
	S3a	8/13/98	S3b	N/O	S3d	11/15/99
			S3c	N/O		
	S4a	8/30/98	S4b	3/1/99	S4c	7/15/99
	S5a	8/30/98	S5b	11/30/98	S5c	9/1/99
	S6a	8/30/98	S6b	3/15/ 7/5/99	S6c	7/15 10/1/99
	S7a	10/23/98	S7b	2/14/99	S7c	10/30/99
Task 2 **Connecting with** **School and Teacher**	C1a	8/31/98	C1b	4/1/99	C1c	8/16/99
	C2a	N/O	C2b	4/1/99	C2c	8/16/99
	C3a	8/30/98	C3b	12/6/98	C3c	8/16/99
	C4a	9/2/98	C4b	2/15/99	C4c	11/3/99
	C5a	12/6/98	C5b	3/28/99	C5c	5/2/99
	C6a	8/30/98	C6c	1/31/99	C6d	6/1/99
	C6b	10/1/98				
	C7a	8/30/98	C7c	1/31/99	C7d	8/15/99
	C7b	10/1/98				
	C8a	9/2/98	C8c	3/28/99	C8d	8/15/99
	C8b	11/30/98				
Task 3 **Relating to Self and** **Others**	R1a	8/30/98	R1b	1/16/99	R1c	
	R2a	N/O	R2b	N/O	R2d	
			R2c	3/16/99		
	R3a	10/1/98	R3b	11/13/99	R3c	5/1/99
	R4a	9/2/98	R4b	3/28/99	R4c	4/28/99
	R5a	9/2/98	R5b	1/30/99	R5c	
			R5c	6/1/99		
	R6a	3/16/99	R6a	3/16/99	R6b	
	R7a	9/2/98	R7b	1/31/99	R7d	
			R7c	2/14/99		
	R8a	8/30/98	R8b	2/14/99	R8d	
			R8c	2/15/99		
	R9a	11/30/98, 12/6/98	R9a	11/30/98	R9b	
	R10a	8/30/98	R10b	12/6/98	R10d	
			R10c	12/6/98		
	R11a	11/30/98	R11a	11/30/98, 12/6/98	R11b	

	0-6 months		6-12 months		12-18 months	
	Subtask	Date	Subtask	Date	Subtask	Date
Task 4 Communicating with Parents, Teachers, and Friends	CM1a	8/30/98	CM1d	11/15/99	CM1e	2/15/99
	CM1b	8/30/98				
	CM1c	10/31/98				
	CM2a	8/30/98	CM2c	12/15/98	CM2e	
	CM2b	11/30/98	CM2d	1/4/99		
	CM3a	9/2/98	CM3c	2/14/99	CM3d	5/1/99
	CM3b	12/15/98				
	CM4a		CM4b		CM4b	
	CM5a	8/31/98	CM5c	2/15/99	CM5d	4/1/99
	CM5b	1/13/99				
	CM6a	2/15/99	CM6b		CM6c	See word list
	CM6b	3/1/99				
	CM7a	1/30/99	CM7b		CM7c	2/14/99
	CM7b	2/14/99			CM7d	5/14/99
Task 5 Moving around Home and School	M1a	8/30/98	M1f	2/15/99	M1k	6/1/99
	M1b	8/30/98	M1g	4/1/99	M1l	8/2/99
	M1c	9/15/98	M1h	5/1/99	M1m	10/1/99
	M1d	11/1/98	M1i	6/1/99	M1n	11/15/99
	M1e	11/19/98	M1j	6/1/99	M1o	10/1/99
					M1p	N/O
	M2a	8/30/98	M2e	12/23/98	M2i	5/14/99
	M2b	10/1/98	M2f	4/1/99	M2j	12/17/99
	M2c	12/23/98	M2g	5/14/99	M2k	
	M2d	1/29/99	M2h	8/14/99		
Task 6 Expressing Feelings with Parents, Teachers, and Friends	E1a	8/30/98	E1b		E1c	
	E2a	9/2/98	E2b	4/1/99	E2c	
	E3a	8/30/98	E3b	3/2/99	E3c	7/15/99
	E4a	9/2/98	E4b	1/31/99	E4c	
	E5a	8/30/98	E5b	2/15/99	E5c	

Index

Innovations

Kay Albrecht and Linda G. Miller

Everything you need for a complete infant and toddler program. The *Innovations* curriculum series is a comprehensive, interactive curriculum for infants and toddlers. Responding to children's interests is at the heart of emergent curriculum and central to the *Innovations* series, which meets the full spectrum of needs for teachers, parents, and the children they care for. In addition to the wealth of activities, each book includes these critical components:

- Applying child development theory to everyday experiences
- Using assessment to meet individual developmental needs of infants and toddlers
- Using the physical environment as a learning tool
- Developing a partner relationship with parents
- Fostering an interactive climate in the classroom
- Educating parents

The *Innovations* series is a unique combination of the practical and theoretical. It combines them in a way that provides support for beginning teachers, information for experienced teachers, and a complete program for every teacher!

Innovations: The Comprehensive Infant Curriculum

416 pages

ISBN 0-87659-213-2 / Gryphon House / 14962 / $39.95

Innovations: The Comprehensive Toddler Curriculum

416 pages

ISBN 0-87659-214-0 / Gryphon House / 17846 / $39.95

Available at your favorite bookstore, school supply store, or order directly from
Gryphon House at 800.638.0928 or www.gryphon house.com

Innovations: Infant & Toddler Development

Kay Albrecht and Linda G. Miller

Understanding infant and toddler behavior can be a challenge. But this **Innovations** book provides teachers with a more thorough understanding of the knowledge base that informs early childhood practice. Focusing on the development of children from birth to age three, **Innovations: Infant and Toddler Development** gives you an in-depth guide to the underlying ages and stages, theories, and best practices of the early childhood field. This enables teachers to begin to address these challenging behaviors in developmentally appropriate ways. 372 pages.

ISBN 0-87659-259-0 / Gryphon House / 19237 / PB / $39.95

Innovations: The Comprehensive Infant & Toddler Curriculum
A Trainer's Guide

Linda G. Miller and Kay Albrecht

The tool every administrator, director, or program manager needs to provide comprehensive training for infant and toddler teachers who are using the **Innovations series (Innovations: The Comprehensive Infant Curriculum** and **Innovations: The Comprehensive Toddler Curriculum)**. Designed to be used as a pre-service model, an in-service model, or as an annual training plan to guarantee well-prepared and trained infant and toddler teachers who plan and implement developmentally appropriate infant and toddler curriculum. 308 pages.

ISBN 0-87659-260-4 / Gryphon House / 15826 / PB / $29.95

Available at your favorite bookstore, school supply store, or order directly from
Gryphon House at 800.638.0928 or www.gryphon house.com

DATE DUE

GAYLORD

PRINTED IN U.S.A.